GOOD FORTUNE
SPELLS

D0204433

INTRODUCTION TO GOOD FORTUNE SPELLS

Magicians have been associated with luck or fortune since magic was first practiced, and the interest it provokes today is evident from the popularity of astrology columns in newspapers and the advertised services of tarot readers and fortune-tellers. We are all conscious of the chances that make a difference in our lives, even those of us who are wise enough to know the huge part that our social situation plays and who do not necessarily subscribe to the idea of a set "fate." Coincidence, synchronicity, or luck—whatever we choose to call it— can set us down paths that lead to life changes. The continued human fascination with these connections stems partly from the notion that magic can manipulate them and contrives to ensure that they manifest in a way favorable to the petitioner.

To a certain extent—the extent to which magic is based on connections, including the synchronicity and coincidences sewn into the great web of life itself—magic can alter the pattern

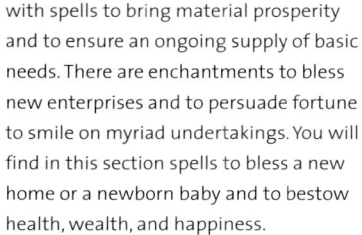

being woven. The spells in this section reflect the ways in which it is possible to weave change to include favorable chance. Many of them are based on very old tools and techniques of magic from around the world. Here you will find traditional spells to help wishes come true or to win your "heart's desire." The customary concerns are also catered to,

with spells to bring material prosperity and to ensure an ongoing supply of basic needs. There are enchantments to bless new enterprises and to persuade fortune to smile on myriad undertakings. You will find in this section spells to bless a new home or a newborn baby and to bestow health, wealth, and happiness.

There are also a number of spells that deal specifically with the issue of luck—both good and bad. These are designed to attract good luck and carry it with you, to "lend" your luck to another—a quaint but time-honored principle of sympathetic magic—and to rid yourself of a run of ill luck. Predictably, there are charms in this section to deal with being *ill-wished*, a folk belief that finds resonance in cultures the world over.

Whatever your needs in the line of fortune, you will find something in this section to suit you. Many of the spells here are based on folk practices from around the world; most of them are eminently adaptable and can be customized to match more specific needs, provided they are based on a similar premise to the original. It is often noted that we make our own fortunes, and to a degree, and for some, this may be true. But sometimes it is good to give ourselves the magical edge to make this possible.

PALINDROME SPELL
TO MAKE A WISH COME TRUE

PURPOSE To secure a favorite wish.

BACKGROUND Palindromes—words that read the same backward as forward—have been used in magical work since ancient times. Remnants of this tradition are found in early Christian magic, which in the first to the third centuries c.e. incorporated many earlier pagan references and traditions. The word ABRACADABRA, invoked by stage conjurers when something amazing is about to happen, actually comes from this

HOW TO CAST THE SPELL

YOU WILL NEED

One charcoal disk in a fireproof dish

Matches or a lighter

Incense made from equal parts orris root, cinnamon, and nutmeg

One dark blue candle, 6–8"/15–20 cm in length

One feather, sharpened to a nib

One bottle of purple ink

One 4"/10 cm square piece of yellow paper

TIMING Perform this working on a waxing moon to draw the wish toward you, on any day. Thursday, ruled by fortunate Jupiter, is the most auspicious day, however.

CASTING THE SPELL

1 Cast a circle in accordance with the guidelines on pages 32–35.

2 Light the charcoal disk, and sprinkle on the incense.

3 Light the candle, saying:
Abraxas, great mage
Mage of mages
Grant me, grant me favor.

tradition and is a mishmash of an earlier palindrome—ABLANATHANALBA. Neither is a true palindrome, but both seem to have been used with good effect for over eighteen hundred years, so this spell will stick to the original!

The principle of the palindrome is not that the word in itself carries any meaning—although remnants found in the late classical period suggest that some may be misspelled deity names—but that the strange quality of the word secures for it a mysterious power. On this basis, palindromes can be used in the form of concrete writing, which shapes words to represent the thing you wish to happen.

In this spell, because we desire something to come to us, we use the palindrome in an increase format—as seen in the early non-true palindrome in the steps below.

When palindromes are used to diminish something, the shape shown is of diminution:

ABRAXARBA
BRAXARB
RAXAR
AXA
X

4 Dip the nib of feather into the ink, and write on the page, in perfectly uniform block letters, the following, while thinking all the while of your wish:

TH
ATHA
NATHAN
ANATHANA
LANATHANAL
BLANATHANALB
ABLANATHANALBA

5 Hold the paper over the incense smoke, and say the lines out loud, beginning with the sound "TH" and working your way down to "ABLANATHANALBA," over and over until the ink is dry.

6 Roll the paper into a scroll, then set it alight by the candle flame and place it on the incense dish to burn, saying:
So my wish is carried to the ether.

LANTERN SPELL
TO OBTAIN YOUR HEART'S DESIRE

PURPOSE To set in motion events that will eventually secure your heart's desire.

BACKGROUND The use of natural ingredients in spells is well established, but sometimes nature surprises us by providing formations that we can exploit for magical means. The physalis (*Physalis peruviana*), sometimes known as Cape gooseberry or Chinese lantern, is one example, producing a beautiful natural formation around its fruit that resembles a lantern. These are buoyant in water and able, if required, to carry and transport small items.

This spell uses the empty lantern of the physalis—which requires removal of the fruit. The physalis "cherries" inside are delightfully scented and taste delicious, so consider this a bonus! The lanterns should be kept as intact as possible in order to keep their buoyancy, because they are to be placed in naturally running water, such as a river or stream, once the spell has been cast.

There is a saying in magic: "Be careful what you wish for." This warning comes because magic may work in unexpected ways, with surprising results. Magic cast upon water is particularly powerful, so ensure your heart's desire is both good and needful.

HOW TO CAST THE SPELL

YOU WILL NEED

One stick of jasmine incense in a holder

Two pale blue candles, 6–8"/15–20 cm in length

Matches or a lighter

One sewing needle

One teaspoon of almond oil

Seven physalis lanterns

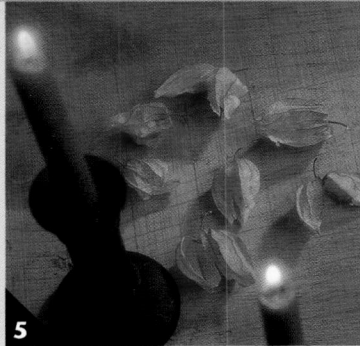

TIMING Cast on a waxing moon to draw your heart's desire, on a Monday, ruled by the moon, patron of our deepest desires.

CASTING THE SPELL

1 Cast a circle in accordance with the guidelines on pages 32–35.

2 Light the incense, then one of the candles, saying:

> To the moon
> All honor
> Pearl of the sky
> Lamp of pale fire
> Hear me and grant
> My heart's desire.

3 With the point of the needle, write on the other candle, from the base to the wick, your heart's desire.

4 Anoint the candle with the oil from the base to the tip and back again twice, then base to tip and halfway down again—avoiding the wick.

5 Light this candle. Open the physalis lanterns, then place a single drop of wax from the candle into each center, once the wax melts around the letter nearest the wick.

6 After the circle, on a waxing moon, launch the lanterns onto natural running water to bear your wishes to the great waters, saying as you launch each:

> So shall it be.

FORTUNA'S WHEEL
TO TURN INDIFFERENT OR BAD LUCK INTO GOOD

PURPOSE To reverse a run of bad luck.

BACKGROUND In medieval Europe the Wheel of Fortune was used to illustrate the fickleness of fate. Sometimes depicted with a king at one side and a beggar at the other, its moral function seems to have been to persuade the poor that their position was divinely ordained. The symbol was actually a corruption of the sacred insignia of a goddess of change, known to the Etruscans as Vortumna, to the Greeks as Tyche, and to the Romans as Fortuna. Her wheel represented the shifting stars, planets, tides, and seasons.

HOW TO CAST THE SPELL

YOU WILL NEED

Five dried basil leaves

One pinch of dried mint

One pinch of saltpeter

One charcoal disk in a fireproof dish

One purple candle, 6–8"/15–20 cm in length

Matches or a lighter

Four long household cook's matches

One 6 ft/1.8 m length of thick purple cotton embroidery thread

TIMING Cast this spell on a waxing moon to move the wheel of Fortuna forward, and on a Thursday, sacred to Jupiter, planet of fair fortune.

CASTING THE SPELL

1 Prior to casting the circle, grind the basil, mint, and saltpeter together.

2 Cast a circle in accordance with the guidelines on pages 32–35.

3 Light the charcoal disk, then the candle, saying:

> *Lady Fortuna*
> *Silver-eyed goddess*

In Wales, the moon, which represents the mysterious powers of nature and magic, was known as Arhianrhod's Wheel—Arhianrhod being a powerful goddess said to weave the fates and fortunes of all. In what is now Germany, pictograms of wheels were carried for luck. The wheel is still used in Hindu and Buddhist iconograph, and is an almost universal symbol of changing fortune.

All of us experience periods in our lives when everything appears to go wrong. If your circumstances seem to be the result of bad luck more than anything else, then this spell is for you.

Turn your wheel for me
And my fortunes bless.

4 Lay the matches across each other at their center to form an eight-spoked wheel with struts of equal length, and fasten them together with one end of the thread.

5 Weave the thread over and under the struts until all the thread is used, beginning from the fastening at the center, chanting:

Weaver, weave in what is best
By the warp and by the weft.

6 Leave sufficient thread by which to hang your wheel above the hearth, and seal it by sprinkling the incense mixture onto the charcoal and censing the wheel in its smoke.

GOLDEN MINT SPELL
TO BRING MATERIAL PROSPERITY

PURPOSE To attract prosperity when it is required for material need.

BACKGROUND Pineapple mint (*Mentha rotundifolia variegata)* is a delightfully scented and delicious member of the mint family. Its variegated leaves, with creamy flecks, lend it a slightly striped effect when it grows en masse in the garden, and its appearance lends variety to the usual greens of mints found in standard herb patches. All varieties of mint are useful in prosperity spells, but pineapple mint, with its golden appearance, is particularly suitable for bringing prosperity from unexpected sources.

As with all prosperity spells, you should be certain to ask for material things for need— this spell will not work if you are lusting after a new model of car or designer clothes. It works on the principle that there is material need involved and will manifest to answer need rather than greed.

Tradition has it that a house with mint growing around it is a house where true riches reside; to pre-industrial peoples this meant, as one old Nordic blessing tells us, food, clothing, shelter, and love. This is perhaps a clue to how this spell works.

HOW TO CAST THE SPELL

YOU WILL NEED

One green candle, 6–8"/15–20 cm in length

One tablespoon of almond carrier oil

Six drops of mint essential oil

Matches or a lighter

One 6"/15 cm length of fine golden cord or ribbon

Six pineapple mint leaves

TIMING Work on a waxing moon to draw prosperity forth, and on any day of the week except Saturday, when restrictive Saturn rules.

CASTING THE SPELL

1 Cast a circle in accordance with the guidelines on pages 32–35.

2 Anoint the candle with the blended carrier and mint oils, avoiding the wick. Cover it from the base to the tip and back six times, then from the base to the tip and halfway back down.

3 Light the candle, saying:
May I prosper as truth prospers
May my fortunes wax as the moon waxes
May my needs be answered as the sea
* answers the shore*
May food, clothes, shelter come as my
* breath comes*
I implore this by the blood of my body
* and the flesh of my bones.*

4 Using the cord or ribbon, fasten the mint leaves together firmly at the stem, and hold them before the candle, saying:
May my vittles, cloth, and roof tiles be as
* plentiful as Mentha in a garden!*

5 Keep your mint leaves in your purse or wallet at all times.

6 Grow mint around your home to maintain the power of this spell.

SPELL OF THREE
TO BLESS A NEW VENTURE

PURPOSE To bring good fortune to a new venture

BACKGROUND Triplicities, or things that come in "threes," have always had an important place in magic. In some cultures, the number three is associated with spirituality. Researchers of the occurrence of the number three in fairy tales have suggested that there may be a strong psychological reason for this. Saying something once awakens the conscious mind; saying it twice makes it unmistakable; and saying it a third time knocks on the subconscious, enabling a thing to be truly known. Repeating things three times in stories must have been a good memory aid for storytellers and

 ## HOW TO CAST THE SPELL

YOU WILL NEED

One yellow candle, 6–8"/15–20 cm in length

Matches or a lighter

One large feather, naturally shed

One small flat disk, 3"/7.5 cm in diameter, of soft self-hardening clay

Three sprigs of fresh rosemary

One 6"/15 cm length of thin red ribbon or wool

One stick of lavender incense in a holder

TIMING To be carried out on a waxing moon and on a Wednesday, day of enterprising Mercury, also associated with the number three.

CASTING THE SPELL

1 Cast a circle in accordance with the guidelines on pages 32–35, in the place where the new venture will be based.

2 Light the candle, saying:
Earth, water, fire combine
Bring blessings to this
   [project/shop/business] of mine
Good fortune in your wheel enshrined.

bards in mainly oral cultures, so there may be something to this theory. In magic, the number three has a particular meaning for the purpose of blessing.

The triskele, on which this spell is based, is found in many Celtic cultures. The one used here comes from Brittany, now a province in northwestern France. Considered to represent the intersection of earth, fire, and water, the triskele is thought to bestow blessings. Druids in North America have based a logo on this design, which sometimes comes with the words: *Beannaithe ag Draoith,* meaning "Blessed by Druids."

3 Using the hard root of the feather, draw the triskele symbol (pictured, right), onto one side of the clay disk.

4 Bind the rosemary sprigs together at the root end with the ribbon or wool.

5 Cense the whole area by carrying the incense and directing the smoke with the rosemary. Now cense the disk in the same way, and set it down to dry hard by the candle.

6 Just before dawn the next day, place the clay triskele disk above the doorway to the premises.

LUCKY HAND SPELL
TO ENSURE GOOD FORTUNE IN ALL YOUR UNDERTAKINGS

PURPOSE To ensure good luck.

BACKGROUND This is a general good luck spell for those who simply want to wish themselves luck, perhaps before setting out on a journey or undergoing a life change. It is based on a blend of traditions—remnants of the medieval Hand of Glory charm and an old English witch custom of "measures." Each are compatible with the aims and methods of sympathetic magic, on which most of the spells in this book are based, and both bring their own powers to bear on this magical working.

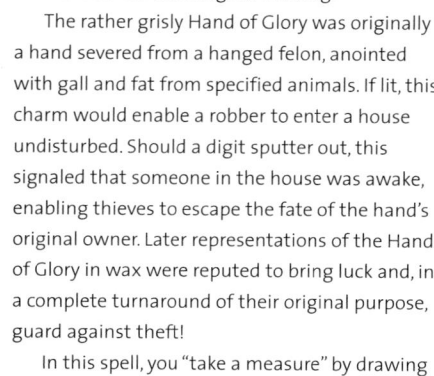

The rather grisly Hand of Glory was originally a hand severed from a hanged felon, anointed with gall and fat from specified animals. If lit, this charm would enable a robber to enter a house undisturbed. Should a digit sputter out, this signaled that someone in the house was awake, enabling thieves to escape the fate of the hand's original owner. Later representations of the Hand of Glory in wax were reputed to bring luck and, in a complete turnaround of their original purpose, guard against theft!

In this spell, you "take a measure" by drawing an outline of your right hand. Witches' measures are still taken by matching cord lengths against a person's own body rather than via a measuring tape, so you are in good magical company if you use this spell!

HOW TO CAST THE SPELL

TIMING Cast this spell on a dark moon, all ready for the growth of the new moon, and on a Thursday, the day of Fortuna, goddess of fortune.

CASTING THE SPELL

1 Cast a circle in accordance with the guidelines on pages 32–35.

2 Light the candle, saying:
Lady Fortuna,
Bless this spell
And my fortune
As well.

3 Rest your right hand, palm down, on the paper. With the pen, draw around the outline of your hand.

4 Write across the paper palm the following:

ROOT
TO
CROWN

Then say:
All held in this palm
Keep from harm,
All here enclosed
Let fortune choose.

5 Cut around the hand outline. Then, say:
I send my wish forth
In smoke

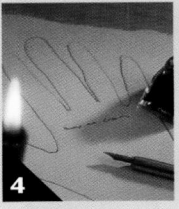
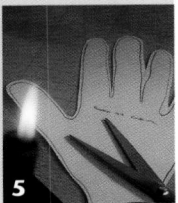

YOU WILL NEED

One dark blue candle, 6–8"/15–20 cm in length

Matches or a lighter

Scissors

One sheet of paper, for drawing around hand

One ink pen with purple ink

One fireproof dish

Set fire to the digits with the candle flame, and place the burning "hand" in the dish to burn completely.

6 Bury the ash in earth, under the night sky, saying:
This wish
In ash
By new moon
Bloom.

MOJO LUCK SPELL
TO ENSURE THAT YOU TAKE LUCK WITH YOU WHEREVER YOU GO

PURPOSE To provide a charm to carry with you at all times.

BACKGROUND The word *mojo* is thought to have come from a word in an African language meaning "magician" or "shaman." A mojo bag is a pouch containing magical items; it may be either a talisman to attract particular powers or an amulet to ward off unwanted energies. Mojo bags and their items are placed together for specific reasons—for example, to turn away the wrath of an enemy or to win the attention of one who will help. Although the mojo bag originates from Afro-American magical

HOW TO CAST THE SPELL

YOU WILL NEED

One charcoal disk in a fireproof dish

Matches or a lighter

Dried juniper berries

One teaspoon of honey

One cream pillar candle, approximately 12"/30 cm high

One spool of red cotton thread

One 3" x 3"/7.5 cm x 7.5 cm red velvet drawstring pouch

One small white pebble

One bunch of dried white sage

TIMING Weave this charm on the sixth night after a new moon, when the moon is visible in the night sky.

CASTING THE SPELL

1 Cast a circle in accordance with the guidelines on pages 32–35.

2 Light the charcoal disk, and sprinkle on the juniper berries.

3 Smear honey onto the top 2"/5 cm of the candle, avoiding the wick. Light the candle saying:

customs practiced in the United States, variations of it exist all over the world. Whether called a mojo, a *gris-gris*, or a charm bag, pouches containing lucky ingredients amount to pretty much the same thing—humans intuitively capturing their luck and carrying it with them.

In this spell, the ingredients are traditional magnets for good luck, based on herbal and craft knowledge, and they should be kept well sealed in your mojo bag, which should be carried with you at all times. The mojo bag makes a good gift for a friend who needs a little luck.

5

Hear me
I stand between the light and the dark
Between a high place and a low place
And none that inhabit these places
May gainsay or cross the luck I seal within.

4 Measure the circumference of your right wrist with the thread. Knot it into a "bracelet" and place it in the pouch.

5 Cense the stone in juniper smoke, and place it in the pouch. Put three sage leaves in the pouch. Light the remaining sage with the candle, and allow it to smolder.

6 Using sage smoke, cense the mojo bag, saying:
All within is pure and safe
That within is that without
That without is that within
Let the charm begin.
Seal the bag immediately.

MOUNTAIN ASH "GOD" SPELL
TO LEND LUCK TO ANOTHER

PURPOSE To be used when you appear to have an excess of good fortune and a friend has none.

BACKGROUND If you consider yourself lucky or blessed, and a friend could use some good luck, this is the spell for you. Obviously, practical advice and material help should come first, but if it genuinely seems that your friend is star-crossed rather than feckless, it is time for magical action. It should be emphasized that casting this spell doesn't mean that your own luck is forfeited. On the contrary, luck, like love, is multiplied when it is shared, and for this reason the recipient should pass on the charm to someone who would benefit from it when their luck turns for the better.

You may have heard people say, when they hear of someone who has been lucky or fortunate, "Maybe their good luck will rub off on me!" In fact, this sort of reaction is the remnant of an old folk belief regarding the ability to pass on luck. The wood of mountain ash (rowan) used in this spell is traditionally referred to as a "god"—itself an indication of much older European beliefs that venerated the spirits and deities of nature within particular trees.

HOW TO CAST THE SPELL

YOU WILL NEED

One green candle, 6–8"/15–20 cm in length

Matches or a lighter

One sharp black-handled kitchen knife

One slim 2"/5 cm length of mountain ash, (rowan) with a fine hole drilled through its side approximately ½"/1 cm from the top to enable a cord to pass through

One 24"/60 cm length of fine cord

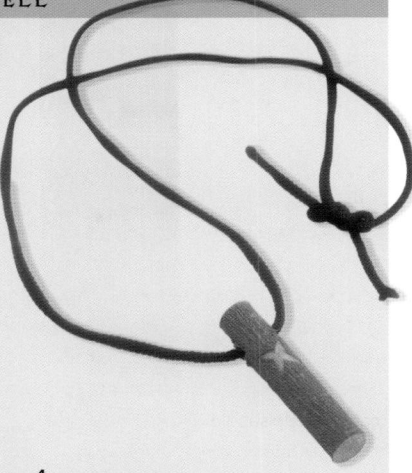

TIMING Work on a waxing moon, and on a Thursday, sacred to Jupiter the generous.

CASTING THE SPELL

1 Cast a circle in accordance with the guidelines on pages 32–35.

2 Light the candle, saying:
God of the earth,
Whose roots drink of water and rock
Whose arms touch the clouds
Bestow your gifts upon [friend's name]
As you have bestowed them upon me
By water, rock, sky, and tree.

3 With the knife, carve into a side of the bark that is at right angles to the drilled hole an X-shaped cross.

4 Spit onto the carved rune, saying:
I gift you by my essence.
Breathe onto it, saying:
I gift you by my breath
I gift you by this god
Good fortune.

5 Pass the mountain ash (rowan) god through the flame, to dry the spittle and seal the spell.

6 Pass the cord through the hole, and wear it as a necklace until you can pass it directly over your friend's head, with a kiss.

EGG SPELL
TO RID YOURSELF OF ILL LUCK

PURPOSE To enable you to cast away bad luck.

BACKGROUND The symbol of the egg has represented, for millennia and across many civilizations, the mysterious essence of life and regeneration. Here, it is used as a symbol of containment and as a way of casting away from you a run of bad luck.

This spell refers to situations that are not of your own making but were arrived at seemingly through a series of chances that have led to a detrimental state of affairs. We sometimes talk of having "a run of bad luck" when we have been relying on luck a little too much. It is important, before casting this spell, that you examine recent events carefully to ensure that it is not a dereliction of responsibility which is responsible for this bad "luck." Otherwise, the spell will be worse than useless, and your bad run will continue.

In the case of circumstances that are genuinely beyond your control and seem to have piled up of late, some magical intervention is entirely legitimate, and the centuries-old tradition behind the Egg Spell is particularly apt to the purpose. It is considered particularly lucky to pass this spell to a friend in need once you have benefited from it.

HOW TO CAST THE SPELL

TIMING Cast this spell on a waning moon, preferably on a Saturday, sacred to Saturn the diminisher.

CASTING THE SPELL

1 Cast a circle in accordance with the guidelines on pages 32–35.

2 Light the black candle, saying:
Your powers that banish
Make ill luck vanish.

3 Bathe the egg in the water, saying:
Your house is clean
When mine is mired
Work ye unto
My desire.

4 Using the needle, make a hole in the narrower end of the egg. Blow into the egg and say:
Ill luck forthwith
From my house
Into thine
From hall of bone
To path of stone,
Get thee hence
From my home
Sprinkle saffron over the hole to seal it.

YOU WILL NEED

One black candle, 6–8"/15–20 cm in length

Matches or a lighter

One free-range chicken egg

Half a wineglass of fresh spring water

One sharp sewing needle

One pinch of saffron

One small-denomination bronze or gold-colored coin

One fresh sprig of yew

5 Take the egg to the garden and dig a hole at least 12"/30 cm deep, then cast in the coin and the sprig of yew. Throw the egg down to smash on them, and cover it quickly with earth.

6 Your luck should change for the better within one moon cycle.

CLOCK SPELL
TO REVERSE THE FORTUNES OF AN ILL-DOER

PURPOSE To frustrate an evildoer in their plans.

BACKGROUND There are many spells in existence that are known as binding or banishing spells (see pages 362–383), and these are often mistaken for "curses." In the sense that they are designed to thwart the nasty ambitions of those who do harm to others, they are; but in the Hollywood B-movie sensationalist media sense, they are not. Bindings and banishings are not performed from spite or for revenge, but to stop harm

HOW TO CAST THE SPELL

YOU WILL NEED

One functioning analog (not digital) clock

One mantelpiece

One black candle, 6–8"/15–20 cm in length

One white candle, 6–8"/15–20 cm in length

Matches or a lighter

One black ink pen

One 4" x 4"/10 cm x 10 cm square piece of black paper

One 81"/202.5 cm length of thick black cotton thread

TIMING Use this spell on a waning moon, on a Saturday, and ensure that it culminates exactly on the stroke of midnight.

CASTING THE SPELL

1 Cast a circle in accordance with the guidelines on pages 32-35.

2 Place the clock in the center of the mantelpiece, the black candle to the left and the white candle to the right.

3 Light the black candle, saying:
May ill deeds be wiped out.
Light the white one, saying:
And good take their stead.

being done. Those doing harm need to learn lessons from their bad behavior, and an adroitly timed spell can do much to bring the consequences of that behavior to their attention.

This spell is a reversal type spell, based on an Anglo-Saxon binding spell. Although it uses the technique of winding the clock backward, its aim is not to turn back time, but to frustrate the designs of an ill-doer. This spell is dedicated to my nephew Joshua Wright, who gave me the idea. The wisdom of children is sometimes beyond measure.

4 Write a large "O" in the center of the paper. Fold it twice, and wrap it with the thread, saying:

The spell I intone
Shall see thee undone
By circle and line
By flesh and by bone
By sea and by sky
By sun and by moon.

5 Turn back the arms of the clock one hour, saying:

For each ill thought
I set thee back.

Turn them back another hour, saying:
For each ill word, I set thee back.
Turn them back another hour, saying:
For each ill deed, I set thee back.
Turn the clock face to the wall.

6 Bury the bound paper deep in your garden, saying:

There you stay until you pay
May wisdom grow
Till good you show.

OAK TREE SPELL
TO ENSURE CONTINUED MATERIAL PROSPERITY

PURPOSE To ensure the continuance of material fortune.

BACKGROUND In Druidic tradition, the oak, closely associated with the element of earth, is also connected with the cycle of the sun. From a magical point of view, these correspondences also coincide with matters of security, fertility, wealth, and health. This makes the oak the ideal tree to call up when you wish to ensure the continued flow of material fortune to your home.

This spell works its magic by means of a magical staff that should be placed at the main doorway to your home. One of the symbols you will carve on it resembles the reverse of the rune known as ken. This rune represents the power of the oak and is set alongside others that magically spell out a charm of security and plenty. This staff should not be fooled around with or handled by anybody outside of your household, or its power will be sapped. Keep it, therefore, out of reach, perhaps on hooks above the doorway. This will ensure that your good work does not go to waste if curiosity gets the better of a visitor to your home!

HOW TO CAST THE SPELL

TIMING Work on a waxing moon, and on a Sunday, ruled by the sun, whose power is embodied by the mighty oak.

CASTING THE SPELL

1 Cast a circle in accordance with the guidelines on pages 32–35. Light the candle, saying:

> *Power of the oak,*
> *Mighty Duir I invoke.*

2 Using the white-handled knife, carve on one side of the staff, about 1 ft/30 cm from the bottom, the symbol *V*, saying:

> *That which is given*
> *None shall shrink.*

3 Carve the symbol of a downward pointing equilateral triangle 6"/15 cm above it, saying:

> *Fortune flowing*
> *None shall sink.*

4 Carve a diamond shape 6"/15 cm above the triangle, saying:

> *Safety in which*
> *To eat and drink.*

5 Finally, 6"/15 cm above the diamond, carve a stave resembling the reverse of the rune ken, saying:

> *Duir forfend*
> *That any send*

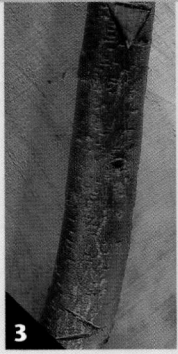
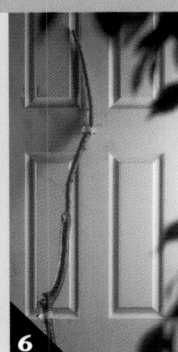

YOU WILL NEED

One green candle, 6–8"/15–20 cm in length

Matches or a lighter

One sharp white-handled knife

One staff of oak, 36"/90 cm in length

One 9 ft/2.7 m length of natural twine

> *A blow or blight*
> *To any wight*
> *That dwells in sooth*
> *Twixt earth and roof.*

6 To seal the magic into the staff, bind it about with twine 2"/5 cm from the top, above the ken rune. Do the same 6"/15 cm from the bottom, below the *V* stave. Hang the stave from your doorway.

TRIANGLE SPELL
TO OBTAIN AN ITEM THAT YOU NEED

PURPOSE To obtain something you genuinely need. This spell will not work if you use it frivolously.

BACKGROUND If you are considering using magic for your own gain, you should always think about what is needful before reaching for your spell book. This is not because of some benighted idea that we should never ask for anything for ourselves, but because in magic, as in any other area of your life, you need to exercise common sense. Expending your energy on spells for things you do not really need means that you are focusing in an imbalanced way on possessions, or people, or invitations that are

HOW TO CAST THE SPELL

YOU WILL NEED

One charcoal disk in a fireproof dish

Matches or a lighter

Dried holly berries

One purple candle, 6–8"/15–20 cm in length

Three x 5"/12.5 cm holly twigs

One 18"/45 cm length of red cotton thread

One 18"/45 cm length of red woolen thread

TIMING Cast on a waxing moon, between the seventh and fourteenth day after the new moon, on any day of the week.

CASTING THE SPELL

1 Cast a circle in accordance with the guidelines on pages 32–35.

2 Light the charcoal disk, and sprinkle on the berries; then light the candle, saying:
   Spirit of the holly tree,
   Come forth as I call to thee.
   Witness all, and let it be.

not, in an essential way, going to do you any good. Besides paying too much attention to these things, the magic itself will not work, except in the sense that bringing an obsession into a magical circle will simply magnify truths about the place it occupies in your life until you deal with it. If you are certain that a thing is both needful and good and that you lack the practical means to obtain it in the usual way, take a chance on this spell. It does yield some unusual results, so be ready for anything! Holly is associated with gifts so your item may come from an unexpected source.

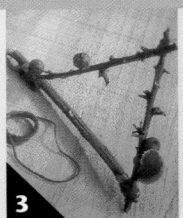

3 Tie the three holly twigs together with cotton thread to form an equilateral triangle with 3"/7.5 cm sides, with the twigs overlapping.

4 Fasten the end of the woolen thread to a corner, then draw it loosely over to another corner and fasten it off. Tie a new length to the third corner, and tie this to the middle of the loose thread to form an equal-armed Y shape in the center.

5 Hold the triangle over the incense, visualizing what you wish for, chanting:

Gift of gifts
Need of need
Leave my dreams
And come to me
As I will it
So mote it be!

6 Hang the triangle from your bedroom ceiling until the wish is fulfilled; then burn it.

LODESTONE SPELL
TO INCREASE MONEY FORTUNE

PURPOSE To attract money wealth.

BACKGROUND The lodestone, or the mineral magnetite, was used historically to cure male sexual dysfunction, to prevent a lover from straying, and to attract money or fortune. It is still used today all over the world for a number of different types of spells, including the very traditional uses already mentioned. Widely available now from crystal and gemstone dealers, lodestones are sometimes painted a color associated with the use to which one wishes to put them. In the United States, for example, it is painted green to attract money—dollar bills being green—in a latter-day variation on sympathetic magic which represents like with like.

In this spell, the lodestone acts as a talisman to attract material fortune in a specifically monetary sense. Generally, spells should focus on final outcomes rather than means to achieve things, and money would normally come under this heading. However, given how often such spells are requested, and in the light of the comprehensive nature of this *Spells Bible*, it would be churlish to leave out such a traditional charm. Suffice it to say that the magical "health" warning of "need, not greed" applies fully here, as elsewhere.

HOW TO CAST THE SPELL

YOU WILL NEED

One green candle, 6–8"/15–20 cm in length

Matches or a lighter

One small lodestone

One saucer of spring water

One teaspoon of iron filings

One teaspoon of almond oil

One 2" x 2"/5 cm x 5 cm brown drawstring pouch

One 24"/60 cm length of fine cord

TIMING Cast on a waxing moon to attract money, and as lodestones are sacred to Venus, work on her day, Friday.

CASTING THE SPELL

1 Cast a circle in accordance with the guidelines on pages 32–35.

2 Light the candle, saying:
Venus, look well
Upon my spell.

3 Hold the lodestone before the candle flame, saying:
Venus, behold one of your children.
Place the lodestone in the water, saying:
Drink well and be strong.

4 Blow onto the stone to dry it; then spoon on the iron filings, saying:
Eat well and be stronger.

5 After about a minute, brush off the filings, and anoint the stone with the almond oil, chanting at least nine times the following rune:
Here is want
Of bright trove
Bring it forth
With your love.

6 Slip the lodestone into the pouch. Fasten it tightly and use the cord to tie into a necklace. Wear the lodestone charm until the needed money appears; then hang it on your bedpost until need arises again, when the spell should be repeated.

LUCKY SHOE-DUST SPELL
TO LEAD YOU INTO GOOD LUCK

PURPOSE To enable luck to walk with you and guide your steps.

BACKGROUND There are many charms that stipulate that they should be placed in someone's shoe, and considering many of the traditions of magic, this is not really surprising. There are many metaphors in Western culture that provide vital clues as to how important feet are considered to be. For example, if we wish to speak of someone putting things into perspective before judging us, we say, "Walk a mile in my shoes, and then judge." When someone takes on the role of another, we speak of them as "stepping into someone else's shoes." We also speak of life directions as "pathways" and of "putting our best foot forward" when we set out on them.

Even though such metaphors appear to be aimed at non-disabled people, those of us who are wheelchair users might wish to note that the importance of the feet from a magical point of view does not begin and end with walking.

Our footprint, whether in sand, or in mud, or in ink, is connected with our "measure"—in witchcraft and magic, something that captures our essence. Accordingly, placing a charm in our shoes is a very powerful magical act.

HOW TO CAST THE SPELL

YOU WILL NEED

Three drops of peppermint essential oil

Thirty drops of carrier oil

One green candle, 6-8"/15–20 cm in length

Matches or a lighter

One yellow candle, 6-8"/15–20 cm in length

One pen with green ink

One sheet of office paper

One fireproof dish

Six dried mint leaves

Six dried basil leaves

TIMING Work on a waxing moon to lead you toward luck, and on a Wednesday, day of wayfaring Mercury.

CASTING THE SPELL

1 Cast a circle in accordance with the guidelines on pages 32-35.

2 Blend the oils, then rub them onto the soles of your feet, saying:
Thus I am guided.
Rub the green candle on your soles, avoiding the wick, and light it.

3 Light the yellow candle, saying:
Traveling in my way
Fortune lead me not astray.

4 Using the green ink, write in the center of the sheet of paper the following words:
Salve Fortuna Salve.

5 Light the paper, using the flame from the green candle, and place it in the fireproof dish to burn completely to ashes. Add the crumbled mint and basil leaves to the cool ash.

6 Mix well by hand, and sprinkle the mixture in both shoes before you next leave your house. Allow it to dissipate naturally.

UNCROSSING SPELL
TO REVERSE BAD LUCK WISHED ON YOU BY ANOTHER

PURPOSE To undo any bad vibes sent your way by the envy or spite of another.

BACKGROUND It is common to hear people say that they are having a run of bad luck, but occasionally they become convinced that their ill fortune is the result of a curse or being wished ill by another. Curses are usually threats made by individuals on ego trips, who imagine that they have magical powers. Happily, the only power these deluded souls have is the power to inflate their own egos. However, envy, spite, and ill feeling carry their own energy, and sometimes you need to feel protected against them.

HOW TO CAST THE SPELL

YOU WILL NEED

One black candle, 6–8"/15–20 cm in length

Matches or a lighter

One small hand mirror

Salt in a pourer

Black cloth

TIMING Cast on the night of the dark moon, which is ideal for breaking spells and building a psychic shield of protection.

CASTING THE SPELL

1 Cast a circle in accordance with the guidelines on pages 32–35.

2 Light the black candle, saying:
What was full is now empty
What was empty is now full
In this time that is not a time
In this place that is not a place
In the world of spirit I stand.

3 On the upward-facing mirror, pour salt in the shape of an X, saying:
Thus I cancel out what is bad.

If you feel you are being "crossed" by someone who wishes you harm, this spell will undo any effects that this ill will might exert, including the anxiety caused by knowing that someone thinks badly of you. It is based on a folk belief, found in many parts of the world, that mixing up your clothing—sometimes turning garments inside out or wearing them back to front—will confuse mischievous powers. After this spell is cast, you should go out of your house at least once a week for a full month with one of your garments either inside out or the wrong way round.

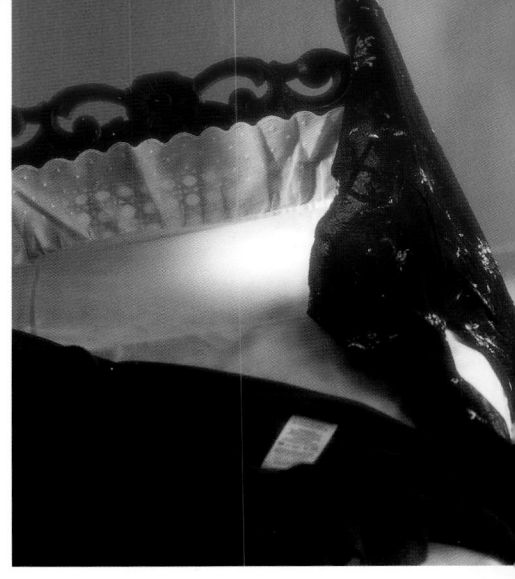

Blow the salt away, saying:
Thus I share out what is good.

4 Take off all your garments. Turn them inside out, and put them on back to front.

5 Pour on the salt in the shape of a circle, with a vertical line through its center, saying:
This moon is empty
This moon is full
Who guesses which
Shall be a fool.

6 Blow away the salt, and wrap the mirror in the black cloth to store in a dark place for a month.

FLAGSTONE SPELL
TO SEND BACK ILL WISHES
TO THEIR ORIGINATOR

PURPOSE To send back ill wishes when you know for sure that a particular person is wishing harm to you or yours.

BACKGROUND In northern European folklore, the flagstone epitomizes all that home and shelter mean to us. These days, most of us have concrete or wooden floors rather than stones inside our homes, so for this spell you will need to find a small paving stone for temporary use. As these are readily available from most home improvement stores or garden centers, this should be neither difficult nor expensive.

Marking patterns on stones is a very old craft, which in parts of the world was once considered an essential part of housekeeping. Cultural historians discovered that the custom of marking front doorsteps with elaborate patterns continued into the twentieth century in Wales. Although pride in the home seemed to be the main motive for these elaborate markings, the curious patterns seem to hark back to the practice of using powerful symbols to protect the household and to claim and identify territory and boundaries. In this spell, you will be marking out boundaries and protecting territory—as well as sending all bad wishes straight back to their originator.

HOW TO CAST THE SPELL

TIMING This spell is best wrought on a dark moon to turn aside bad intent. Renew it every three months for the first year by chalking over the markings on December 21, March 21, June 21, and September 21.

CASTING THE SPELL

1 Cast a circle next to your front door in accordance with the guidelines on pages 32–35.

2 Stand the candle directly in the center of the stone, using molten wax to stabilize it.

3 Draw a chalk arrow appearing to go through the candle, pointing left.

4 Place the stone before your front door, saying:

Thus have you injured.

Turn it around so that the arrow points out the front door, saying:

I put you to rout
As I turn you about.

5 In the top left-hand corner, draw a small square, saying:

Hearth.

In the top right-hand corner, draw an X, saying:

Love.

YOU WILL NEED

One black candle, cut down to 3"/7.5 cm in length

Matches or a lighter

One square paving stone, 8–12"/20–30 cm square

One thick piece of chalk

In the bottom left-hand corner, draw an upward pointing arrow, saying:

Roof above.

In the bottom right-hand corner, draw a circle with a dot in the center.

6 Allow the candle burn down, then cover the stone with a rug, and keep it by your front door.

KITCHEN WITCH SPELL
TO ENSURE THAT YOU AND YOURS WILL NEVER GO HUNGRY

PURPOSE To create a lucky charm to ensure that your household will never go short of food.

BACKGROUND The kitchen witches sold in shops in the United States and in parts of Europe are often figures of cute old grannies on broomsticks, which advertisers claim will ensure that your cooking does not get spoiled. In fact, the idea behind these wall charms originated in Europe, where salt dough figures were used to contain the spirit of the corn cut from the previous harvest. Preserving the flour in this way was

HOW TO CAST THE SPELL

YOU WILL NEED

One red candle, 6–8"/15–20 cm in length

Matches or a lighter

Household salt, one cupful

Plain white flour, one cupful

Water, one cupful

One large bowl

One egg white

One teaspoon of poppy seeds

One oven

One 12" x ½"/30 cm x 1 cm length of red ribbon

TIMING Cast this spell on a waxing moon, as near to full as possible.

CASTING THE SPELL

1 Cast a circle in your kitchen in accordance with the guidelines on pages 32–35. Set your oven to 100°F/38°C.

2 Light the red candle and, passing your hands on each side of the flame back and forth three times, say:
I invoke the spirit of life,
I invoke the spirit of earth.

thought to ensure the return of the corn spirit for the next crop. At some point, the dough came to be baked in the shape of good witches, ostensibly to frighten off so-called bad witches who might spoil the corn.

The salt dough figure of this spell will not demand much of your artistic abilities, as it invokes the original symbolism of the salt dough—to ensure plenty. Your kitchen witch may not have a pointy hat or broom, but rest assured that she is far more powerful than the "cute old lady" figures currently on the market!

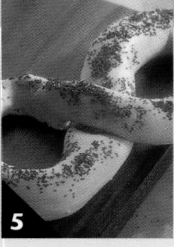

3 Place the salt and flour in the bowl and blend, then add water until the dough is smooth and pliant. Knead for at least three minutes, chanting the following words:

Come wealth, come weal
Come plenty by.

4 Roll the dough into an even tube, and form it into a figure eight.

5 Coat it with egg white, and press the poppy seeds evenly into the surface. Place it in the oven. The dough is cooked if it sounds hollow when rapped. Cooking times differ from oven to oven, so check it frequently. When the cooking is complete, allow it to cool.

6 Dress it with a red bow, and hang it in your kitchen.

ROMAN CORNUCOPIA SPELL
TO BESTOW LUCK ON A NEW HOME

PURPOSE To bring luck to a new home—ideal for blessing a couple moving into their first home together.

BACKGROUND The symbol of the cornucopia, or "horn of plenty," appears from Renaissance times in Western art to signify abundance. It was originally an ancient Roman symbol of a magical horn that held an endless supply of food. This was usually seen carried by a goddess figure in Roman religious art and was so popular that a number of deities became associated with it: Abundantia (abundance), Spes (hope), Copia (wealth), Ceres (growth), Justitia (justice), and Concordia (peace) were all seen with this symbol. The frequency with which it appears in ancient times—and its ongoing popularity as a necklace charm—perhaps reflects the perennial concerns of humans with ensuring a sufficiency of resources.

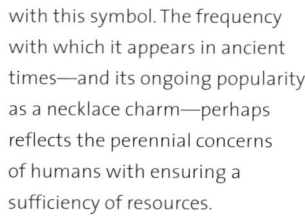

Another custom that the ancient Romans left us is closely connected with the cornucopia. This is the act of bestowing bread, oil, and salt on a new household in order to guarantee that none of these staples is lacking in the future. This spell is based on that ritual and uses the ancient symbol of the cornucopia to draw good luck to the home.

HOW TO CAST THE SPELL

TIMING Work with a waxing moon to ensure that resources flow into your home, and on any day of the week apart from Saturday, domain of frugal Saturn.

CASTING THE SPELL

1 Cast a circle in accordance with the guidelines on pages 32–35.

2 Light the candle, saying:
I call upon Ceres
Goddess of the corn harvest
Of fertility and growth
To witness and bless this spell.

3 Cut the roll in half, and spoon the oil into the center of one side, saying:
May goodness flow here.
Sprinkle the salt into the other side, and repeat the line above.

4 Tie the halves together again with twine, and fasten off, saying:
All that is needful is sealed in this house.
Fold the felt into an open cone, stitching with the thread to secure it.

5 Place the bread into the cone, and sew the top flap shut.

6 Keep this in your own home, or present it to friends when entering their home, saying:
What abundance has made
Abundance will bless.

YOU WILL NEED

One green candle, 6–8"/15–20 cm in length

Matches or a lighter

One sharp knife

One small bread roll

One teaspoon of virgin olive oil

One pinch of salt

One 18"/45 cm length of twine

One 12"/30 cm square piece of red felt

One spool of red thread

One sewing needle

RED BRACELET SPELL
TO BESTOW GOOD FORTUNE ON A NEWBORN BABY

PURPOSE To weave a charm to bring luck to a newborn.

BACKGROUND Cords and threads are important in magic, never more so than when they represent life and destiny. In this spell, a variation on a custom found in various parts of the world, they signify the future fortunes of a newborn and are therefore to be treated with great respect. Anthropologists have often noted the emphasis placed on cords in various rites of passage in many cultures, and tying a lucky wristband on a newborn is a common custom all over the world. Traditions where a red thread is employed use the color to signify power, health, and long life, and these themes are taken up in this charm, which has a distinctly Celtic flavor.

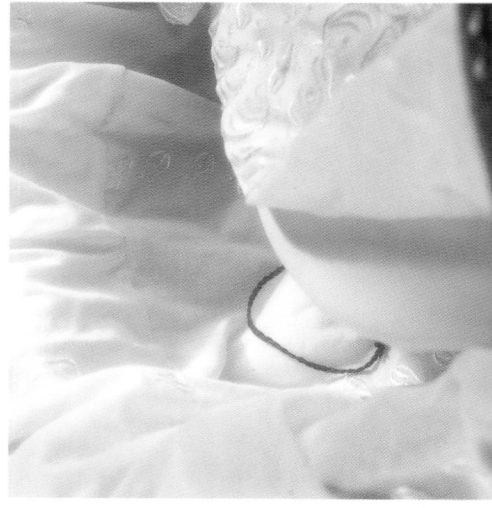

In Celtic beliefs, the goddess Brigid is a protector of all newborn creatures. In her triple aspect, she is healer, bringer of fire, and inspiration of both poets and craftspeople. She is closely associated with triplicities—things that come in threes—and sometimes is seen depicted with braided knot work decorating her attire or framing her image. Here, she is invoked to bless and empower with good fortune a braided red bracelet to give to a newborn.

296

HOW TO CAST THE SPELL

YOU WILL NEED

One charcoal disk in a fireproof dish

Matches or a lighter

Three red candles, 6-8"/15–20 cm in length

Three 18"/45 cm lengths of 15-thread thick red embroidery skein

One pencil

Three teaspoons of frankincense

Scissors

One eggcup of water

One pinch of salt

TIMING Work on a waxing moon to attract good fortune, and on a Sunday, in honor of fiery Brigid.

CASTING THE SPELL

1 Cast a circle in accordance with the guidelines on pages 32–35.

2 Light the charcoal disk.

3 Light three candles. After lighting each one, say the following in turn:

Brigid, queen of healing wells. (Candle 1)
Brigid, queen of balefires. (Candle 2)
Brigid, queen of makers
Hail and welcome. (Candle 3)

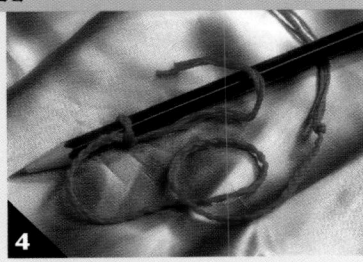

4 Tie the strands to a pencil, and weave a braid, chanting the following throughout:

Your days be long
Your shadow great
Your heart be glad.

Fasten, and cut when the braid is 4"/10 cm longer than the baby's wrist measurement.

5 Sprinkle incense on the charcoal, and pass the braid through the smoke, saying:

Air to speed you fortune.

Pass it through candle heat, saying:

Fire to haste you power.

Sprinkle it with water, saying:

Water to bring you love.

Sprinkle it with salt, saying:

Earth to send you health
And Brigid walk with you in your
footsteps.

6 Tie the bracelet around the baby's wrist; then remove it, and place it under the crib mattress.

BERRY NECKLACE SPELL
TO BRING HEALTH, WEALTH, AND HAPPINESS

PURPOSE To bless you with health, wealth, and happiness.

BACKGROUND Berries are versatile ingredients, used in incense blends and potions. Their traditional symbolism is employed in spell work, and they carry magical energies. They also look attractive when used in charms to be hung in the home! This charm draws on traditions associated with mountain ash (rowan), juniper, and holly berries and uses their magical vibrations in charm for health, wealth, and happiness.

 HOW TO CAST THE SPELL

YOU WILL NEED

One red candle, 6–8"/15–20 cm in length

One green candle, 6–8"/15–20 cm in length

Matches and a lighter

One 48"/120 cm length of black thread

One sharp needle

One bowl

Dried juniper berries, 4 oz/115 g

Dried berries of mountain ash (rowan), 4 oz/115 g

Dried holly berries, 4 oz/115 g

TIMING Work on a waxing moon, and on Tuesday, sacred to protective Mars.

CASTING THE SPELL

1 Cast a circle in accordance with the guidelines on pages 32–35.

2 Light the red candle, saying:
   Health and heart prevail.
Light the green candle, saying:
   Wealth and weal, all hail.

4 Thread the needle, doubling the thread.

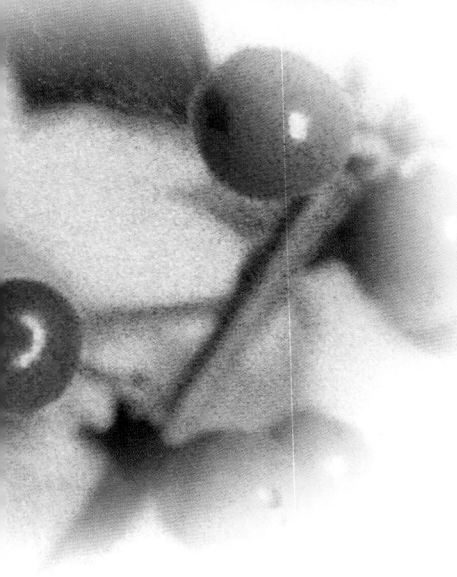

In tree lore, mountain ash (rowan) and juniper ward off evil, and their berries have particularly protective properties. They are used in purification and protection incense blends, and will ward off thieves when kept by the back door of a house. The holly tree has a similar reputation, although its berries are accredited with the power to bind oaths and seal lover's pledges. Among the more arcane properties of all three are the abilities to ensure health, plenty, and happiness. This spell calls on these lesser-known influences to empower a charm designed to attract all three.

5 Pour the juniper berries into the bowl, and with your hands palm down on them, say:
> *Berries in your house of black*
> *Never hold your bounty back.*

Repeat with the berries of mountain ash (rowan), saying:
> *Mountain ash in your house of blood*
> *Keep me hale and do me good.*

Repeat with the holly berries, saying:
> *Holly berries, for my sake*
> *Happy find and merry make.*

6 Thread the berries onto the thread in the order outlined above, chanting:
> *Three bright things I would possess*

> *Health, wealth, and happiness*
> *Health show, wealth grow*
> *Happiness all in this row.*

When the thread is full, tie the ends together, and pass it over your head. Walk to the heart of your house, and hang the necklace from the highest point.

PROTECTION AND BLESSING SPELLS

INTRODUCTION TO PROTECTION AND BLESSING SPELLS

The power to bless and protect has been both valued and feared in Western societies for several centuries. This is because the nature of magic itself has been largely misunderstood. Rituals and charms for blessings and protection have sometimes been assumed to be absolute: that a person or object once blessed is totally impervious to the harms of the world. This is a dangerous assumption to make, both for those who believe themselves invincible through magic and particularly for those who perform the spells, as they are consequently blamed when things go wrong. It is this latter tendency that has, in past times, led to accusations of "cursing" or even "killing" when the intention has been to protect or heal.

Fear and misapprehension about the magical ability to protect or bless arise from the mistaken belief that with the ability to bless comes also the ability to curse. This has encouraged fear and loathing of magical folk and, in times

gone by, persecution. Thinking of this type comes from a mindset—a very common one—that sees all aspects and principles of existence in black and white and divides the world into positive–negative opposites. Magic, however, does not operate according to such principles, and spells for protection and blessing are exactly what they say they are!

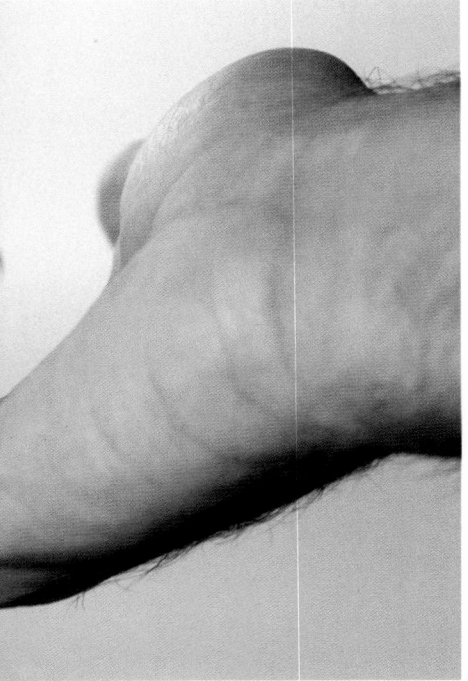

Rites for protection are not curses but ways of harnessing the power of magic to provide safeguards and to discourage the dishonest, spiteful, or deceitful from doing harm. Similarly, blessings are not fail-safe devices that keep the arrogant and foolish from harm. Rather, they should be seen as messages sent into the magical web by someone who respects the power of spirit and who wishes blessings to come to them or to another who is deserving.

Be reassured that the blessing spells in this section are not the flip side of another, more sinister aspect of magic, and moreover, that by invoking protection, you are not cursing anyone. The foci of the spells in this section should set your mind at rest on this count, as you will find spells to bless your home or a newborn baby and to wish a couple well in their life together. You will also find charms and magic to protect your home against intrusion and theft, to combat deceit in others, to fend off unwanted attentions, and to deflect spite.

To close this section, you will find a very special blessing, well known to witches, that helps you to gather your strength and face adversity in times of trouble.

MEXICAN EYE SPELL
TO GUARD AGAINST THE EVIL EYE

PURPOSE To deflect ill wishes.

BACKGROUND The *Ojo de Dios*, or "Eye of God," symbol used in this spell is a protective device of ancient origin. The Huichol people of Mexico wove this symbol as a means to fend off evil and invite supernatural protection. Similar artifacts for the same purpose have been found in other parts of South America as well as in Africa and the East. The Eye of God is depicted in different ways in art—one common depiction is a round eye with a horizontal iris surrounded by a sunburst—but the simplest and most common representation is seen in woven specimens similar to that created in this spell.

HOW TO CAST THE SPELL

YOU WILL NEED

One charcoal disk in a fireproof dish

One orange candle, 6–8"/15–20 cm in length

Matches or a lighter

One teaspoon of frankincense

Two oak twigs 8"/20 cm in length

Balls of wool in the following colors: black; red; orange; yellow; green; turquoise; azure

One pinch of cinnamon

TIMING Cast this spell on a Sunday to honor the patron of the spell, and on a waxing moon, to draw its strength.

CASTING THE SPELL

1 Cast a circle in accordance with the guidelines on pages 32–35.

2 Light the charcoal, then the candle, saying:

> *Mighty Sol*
> *All-seeing eye*
> *Light upon all enemies*
> *Who dwell beneath sky*
> *Find them out,*
> *Put evil to rout.*

Belief in *the evil eye*, or the ability to cause harm to someone by looking at them with ill intent, is found all over the world. Often it is the fear of such power that does the job of any curse or ill wish, as worrying and fretting about curses simply gives them a bigger space in your life. But it is easy to tell someone not to fret and hard for them to ignore their fears, so this spell concentrates the mind toward feelings of security by invoking the protection of the sun. While you are weaving your *Ojo de Dios,* try chanting or humming to raise the magical vibes and strengthen the spell.

 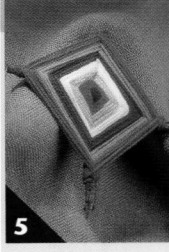

3 Sprinkle the frankincense onto the charcoal.

4 Place the twigs across each other at right angles, and fasten them at the center with black wool.

5 Weave nine rounds of each color in the order outlined above, drawing the wool under and around each of the four struts in succession, so that the wool wrapped around the twigs stands out against that which is woven between.

6 When you are finished, fasten off securely. Place the cinnamon on the charcoal, and cense your Eye of God in the smoke, saying:
   I seal and proclaim you
   Let none defame you.
Hang it over your bed.

SNAPDRAGON SPELL
TO GUARD AGAINST SPITE

PURPOSE To protect against the spiteful intents of others.

BACKGROUND The snapdragon, or *Antirrhinum majus*, is a flower beloved of children, who pinch the base of the blossoms to make the "dragon mouth" of the bloom snap open and shut. It has the reputation of being highly protective of the pure in heart and is particularly powerful in fending off the spiteful intentions of others. The flowers, which are highly popular with bees, are diverse in color, and the most exciting hues are perhaps the fiery yellows and reds—real dragon colors!

As a child, I found this flower in the front gardens of houses I passed on the way to one of the city parks. My friends and I would dare each other to pick blossoms from the plants. I was pleased to discover, when I grew up to have children of my own, that youngsters are still fascinated with snapdragons and can still be seen roaring around and chasing each other with the snapping maws of the flowers. It seems that little children know instinctively where magic lies!

HOW TO CAST THE SPELL

TIMING Cast this spell on a waning moon to repel, and on a Tuesday, day of fierce and fiery Mars.

CASTING THE SPELL

1 Cast a circle in accordance with the guidelines on pages 32–35.

2 Light the charcoal, then the red candle.

3 Heat the point of the nail in the candle flame; then use it to etch an upward-pointing equilateral triangle into the side of the candle 1"/2.5 cm from the wick.

4 Sprinkle the rosemary onto the charcoal.

5 Place snapdragon blossoms into the pouch one by one, reciting the following lines, one to each as you do so:

Power of one, the mighty sun
Power of two, hold right and true
Power of three, sting of the bee
Power of four, all harm deplore
Power of five, voice of the hive
Power of six, all harm desist
Before the seven, all harm be driven.

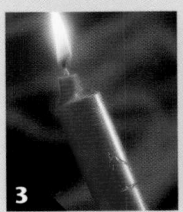 3

 6

YOU WILL NEED

One charcoal disk in a fireproof dish

One red candle, 6–8"/15–20 cm in length

Matches or a lighter

One sharp masonry nail

One teaspoon of dried rosemary

Seven snapdragon blossoms

One 2" x 2"/5 cm x 5 cm red drawstring pouch

One 24"/60 cm length of fine cord

5 Hold the pouch between your palms, and visualize its power as dragon fire, ready to blast all spite and unkindness that comes near. Pass the pouch through the incense smoke to seal it.

6 Attach the cord and wear the pouch around your neck for personal protection, or hang it in your home to guard your family or housemates.

HERB GUARDIAN SPELL
TO PROTECT YOUR HOME
FROM BURGLARY AND THEFT

PURPOSE To deter thieves.

BACKGROUND Evidence of charms to guard against theft dates back centuries, and traditions relating to house guardians go back thousands of years. Many old spells relating to repelling thieves refer to herbal knowledge and magical and religious

symbolism. However, the principle of creating a guardian for the home is informed by a magical technique sometimes called god-making. This spell comprises both herbal and god-making techniques.

Juniper berries, well known in magic for their power to dispel evil intentions, are also regarded as safeguards against theft. Here, a berry is placed inside a small wax figure into which you will also place your intent to deflect all thieves. Since the juniper berry will form its "heart," you can be assured that the sole reason for the guardian you create will be to protect your home and property. For this spell you will need to construct a mold of modeling clay in which to cast the figure to be your Herb Guardian. Since one of the arms (the right) is to carry a miniature sword, you will need to make it thick enough to be pierced by a needle without actually breaking any of the arm away. This will mean some prior preparation and perseverance.

HOW TO CAST THE SPELL

TIMING Perform your work on a waning moon, on a Saturday, dedicated to Saturn the banisher.

CASTING THE SPELL

1 Before casting the circle, prepare the modeling clay by forming a mold for a humanoid figure approximately 4"/10 cm high, and place it on the plate. Prepare the wax by placing the jar in a pan of boiling water on a heated burner on the stove; put the candles in the jar and let them melt.

2 Cast a circle in accordance with the guidelines on pages 32–35.

3 Light the black candle, saying:
As Saturn's rings surround the whole
My guardian protect this home.

4 Pour the wax into the mold and sprinkle it with sage. Chant while you are waiting for it to solidify:
Evil deed and evil word
All are banished by your sword.

5 When the wax is almost set, place the juniper berry where the heart would be. Place the eye end of the needle into the "hand" of the figure, with the point jutting out.

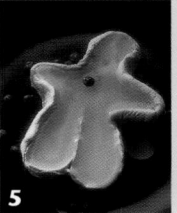

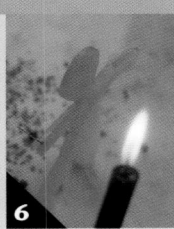

YOU WILL NEED

One large ball of soft modeling clay

One heatproof plate

One glass jar

One pan of boiling water

Twelve household candles

One black candle, 6–8"/15–20 cm in length

Matches or a lighter

One teaspoon of chopped sage

One juniper berry

One sewing needle

6 When the figure is completely solidified, cease chanting. Extinguish the candle, and bury the guardian near your property, sword pointing outward with the candle by its side.

SWORD SPELL
TO PROTECT AGAINST ALL TYPES OF INTRUSION

PURPOSE To defend against intrusion. This spell has long been used by witches to defend their homes and meeting places.

BACKGROUND The central technique of this spell is one that is used to a greater or lesser extent in many spells: that of visualization. If you were ever accused of daydreaming when you were a child, there is a good chance that you will have a flair for visualization in a magical context. In magic, visualization techniques are valuable because they help you to focus on the purpose of the spell and at the same time to empower it with your intent. An advanced form of this technique is creating a thought-form to do your bidding.

When we use a thought-form that resembles ourselves (a feature of mirror magic) it is known as a *fetch*. However, in this spell, you are creating a body of energy in the form of an object—a sword, the archetypal symbol of defense. It is a simple technique, but it requires concentration and self-discipline. It would be a good idea, therefore, to spend some time practicing the technique of visualization in a cast circle until you are confident that you can hold your concentration for the purposes of this spell.

HOW TO CAST THE SPELL

YOU WILL NEED

One charcoal disk in a fireproof dish

Matches or a lighter

Nine tea-lights in secure holders

One teaspoon of mugwort

One teaspoon of dittany of Crete

TIMING Work on a dark moon to empower this spell.

CASTING THE SPELL

1 Cast a circle in accordance with the guidelines on pages 32–35.

2 Light the charcoal.

3 Sit on the floor in the center of the circle, facing north, and place the tea-lights at equal points in a circle around you before lighting them.

4 Sprinkle mixed mugwort and dittany onto the charcoal, and breathe in the scent.

5 Close your eyes, slow your breathing, and allow yourself to drift into the darkness within. When you are ready, envisage in the north of the circle a shield; in the east a wand; in the south a sword; and in the west a chalice. Allow the shield, wand, and chalice images to merge into that of the sword. Envisage the sword passing over your head to the front of you, resting point downward. Now mentally instruct the sword to guard your home, and set it spinning in a vertical arc. Mentally move this spinning sword toward the front boundary of your home.

6 To ensure that its strength is continually renewed, envisage the sword spinning in this place prior to going to sleep each night.

HERB CORSAGE SPELL
PROTECTION AGAINST UNWANTED ATTENTIONS

PURPOSE   To fend off all uninvited attentions.

BACKGROUND   There are many spells to attract suitors, or the attention of influential work colleagues, and to make new friends. Because life is complicated, magical tradition also provides us with the magical means to deflect attention away from ourselves, when it is unwanted and uninvited. This spell, designed to repel unwanted notice, can be used for many purposes. It could be that you have an unwanted suitor or that you wish to escape the attentions of a bully or an unpleasant personality. This spell cannot render you invisible in given situations—let's face it, no one with a bunch of herbs in their lapel is ever going to be invisible—but the power of the herbs and your stated intentions are wielded to repel those you wish to avoid. Wearing the Herb Corsage charm created by this spell is to declare magically the wish

that the person or persons you are evading will pass by without invading your private space. "Wearing your heart on your sleeve" is a saying that applies to anyone who leaves themselves vulnerable by making obvious to all where their heart lies. Wearing these herbs on your lapel is to guard your own heart and your integrity and make your thinking clear on the matter:
Stay away!

HOW TO CAST THE SPELL

YOU WILL NEED

One red candle (for Mars) or one black candle (for Saturn), each 6–8"/15–20 cm in length

Matches or a lighter

One sprig of white heather

One sprig of thyme

One 9"/22.5 cm length of natural twine

One ball of absorbent cotton

One saucer of water

One twist of aluminum foil

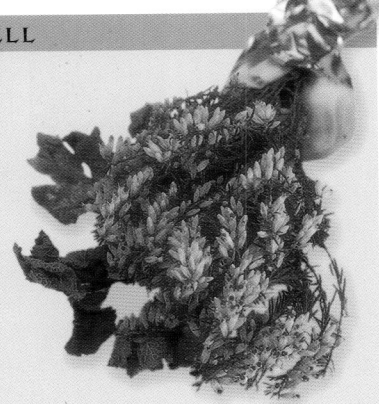

TIMING A waning or dark moon is best for this spell, and Saturday, for stern Saturn, or Tuesday, day of fiercely defensive Mars, are the most favorable days.

CASTING THE SPELL

1 Cast a circle in accordance with the guidelines on pages 32–35.

2 Light the candle, saying:
[Mars/Saturn], you are honored here
Let no enemy near
Whose notice I fear.

3 Bind the heather and thyme stems together with twine. Dip the absorbent cotton in the water and squeeze it out, then apply it to the roots of the thyme and heather. Cover the absorbent cotton with foil.

4 Hold the corsage before the candle flame, visualizing the person or persons you wish to avoid passing you by, as if they had been repelled.

5 Repeat the following incantation nine times over the corsage:
Cardea
Ouvret
Allaya
Dixet.

6 Wear the herb corsage on your lapel until it dies off; then dry the herbs and crumble them into an open fire to seal the spell.

TRISKELION SPELL
TO PROTECT A TRAVELER

PURPOSE To protect you on your travels.

BACKGROUND The word *triskelion* comes from the Greek and means "three-legged." It is a very old symbol that has been ascribed many meanings through the ages and that is inevitably bound up with the mysterious nature of triplicities. The triskelion in this spell draws on the Manx legend with which it is most associated, to provides travelers with a charm that will help them bounce back should they encounter difficulties on their journey.

Ellan Vannin, or the Isle of Man, is well known for its mix of Viking and Celtic history. Its chief insignia, the triskelion, has its origins in the mists of time—the earliest

HOW TO CAST THE SPELL

YOU WILL NEED

One pale blue candle, 6–8"/15–20 cm in length

Matches or a lighter

One small single scallop shell, drilled

One fine paintbrush

One tube of vermilion oil paint

One 24"/60 cm length of fine black cord

TIMING Cast on a waxing moon and on a Sunday, sacred to the sun.

CASTING THE SPELL

1 Cast a circle in accordance with the guidelines on pages 32–35.

2 Light the candle, saying:
Mannanan of the waters
Mannanan the traveler
Look well upon [name]
That they are hale going out
And hale coming in.

3 Paint on the inside of the scallop shell the outline of a triskelion.

depictions of this sign are found in prehistoric rock carvings in Italy—but it is linked to a most intriguing legend. The magician Manannan guarded the island with magical mists. Sensing the coming of Christianity and the new age that was at hand, he turned his followers into triskelions and rolled them down Snaefell, the Isle of Man's highest mountain, and into the sea, to dwell in a kingdom beneath the waves. This tale of transformation and survival gave the Manx their motto: *Quocunque Jeceris Stabit*, which Manx folk prefer to translate as "However you throw us, we stand."

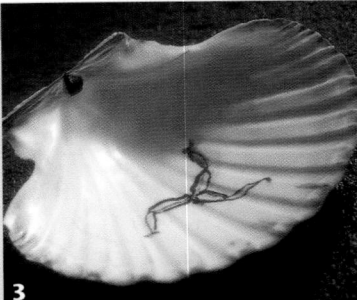

4 Sit in the center of the circle with the upturned shell in your upturned right palm, which should be placed over your upturned left palm. Close your eyes, and visualize the triskelion you have painted spinning clockwise, faster and faster until it is a blur.

5 When you are ready, blow onto the shell with your breath to bless it with the power of air. When the paint dries, thread it with the cord, and dip it into natural saltwater at the earliest opportunity.

6 The triskelion pendant should be worn around the neck of those who would call on its protective powers.

WITCHWOOD SPELL
TO DISPEL EVIL INTENT

PURPOSE To drive evil away.

BACKGROUND Mountain ash (rowan) is considered by magicians to offer magical protection of the highest order. There are many old country sayings and saws relating to mountain ash, nearly all of them referring to the mountain ash's power to dispel evil and protect bearers of the wood from harm. Apparently, mountain ash trees keep witches away, this belief coming from a time when the word *witch* was synonymous with evil. However, witches, who have never yet been "kept away" by mountain ash, tend to refer to it as *witchwood* precisely because of its reputation for goodness!

Mountain ash are wonderful trees that grow very quickly if planted in groves with other trees, making them good protection for saplings of slower-growing trees that are less hardy. They like lots of air and light and are often found growing in high places; they are common in the Scottish Highlands. They live up to two hundred years and are less prone to disease and breakage than many other trees. This hardiness makes them an appropriate symbol of endurance and protection.

HOW TO CAST THE SPELL

YOU WILL NEED

One charcoal disk in a fireproof dish

One red candle, 6–8"/15–20 cm in length

Matches or a lighter

One 2"/5 cm section of a small branch of mountain ash, drilled through ½"/1 cm from the top

One sharp whittling knife

One 36"/90 cm length of red wool thread

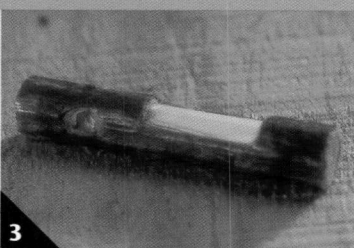

TIMING Cast this spell on a dark moon in the Fall to grow your protective shield. Cull a small branch and seal the raw edge.

CASTING THE SPELL

1 Cast a circle in accordance with the guidelines on pages 32–35.

2 Light the charcoal, then the candle. Cut a 4"/10 cm strip of wool, and burn it over the flame, saying:

As this flame dissolves this thread
Mountain ash wood shall deal all dread.

3 Whittle away the bark, and place it on the charcoal to smolder. Cut away a strip of the wood to just below the drilled hole, making a flat surface.

4 Cut into this surface an upward-pointing equilateral triangle with a horizontal line through the center.

5 Hold the pendant over the smoking bark, saying:

All good enter in
All evil to flee
Within my good hand
All evil withstand.

6 Wind the thread three times around the top of the charm, and secure it; then thread it through the drilled hole, forming a pendant to be worn around the neck.

DAEG RUNE SPELL
TO COMBAT DECEIT

PURPOSE To help you see clearly through lies and deceit.

BACKGROUND *Daeg*, the rune on which this spell is based, is one of the eight symbols representing the last third of the ancient twenty-four character runic script. This group of runes is known as *Tyr's aett* and is the set most associated with human matters and characteristics. As Tyr is a god of justice and a great defender against wrongs, all of these runes have something of his nature in them. In the case of daeg, literally "day" or "daylight," the wrongs to be fought are related to deceit and the need to see things clearly.

As we go through life, there is a tendency to trust less after we have experienced deceit. Sometimes this is what is needed, for as the saying goes: "If a man deceive me once, shame on him. If he deceive me twice, shame on me." However, sometimes we need a little help in training our instincts, and this is where the Daeg Rune Spell comes in.

Daeg represents clear seeing and our ability to turn our understanding around 180° where necessary. This rune is also associated with necessary change. All of this makes daeg the ideal rune to call on when you wish to guard yourself from the deceits of others.

HOW TO CAST THE SPELL

3 Take the chalk, and draw the rune daeg onto the piece of slate or stone. Pour the salt in an unbroken line, tracing it over the chalk marks you have made.

4 Hold this up before the candle, saying:

> *Let it be uncovered*
> *That which was hidden*
> *And [name of potential deceiver] tell*
> *   the truth*
> *As [she/he] is bidden.*

5 Blow away the salt, and show the chalked rune to the candle flame.

6 Place the chalked rune outside until the rain washes it away. You should discover the truth of the matter within three moon cycles.

YOU WILL NEED

One gold orange candle, 6–8"/15–20 cm in length

Matches or a lighter

One stub of white chalk

One coaster-size (minimum) piece of slate or stone

One container of salt with a flow hole

TIMING Cast on a waxing moon, on a Sunday, day of the all-seeing sun.

CASTING THE SPELL

1 Cast a circle in accordance with the guidelines on pages 32–35.

2 Light the candle, and whisper the name of the person you think may be deceiving you, close enough to the flame to make it flicker.

HERB POPPET SPELL
TO PROTECT AGAINST HARDSHIP

PURPOSE Cast this spell to guard against privation.

BACKGROUND This spell uses a poppet (sometimes referred to as a *fith-fath*), a very old magical technique that embodies a wish or a person. A poppet is a stuffed figure made from two sections of cloth that are cut to a roughly humanoid shape, then sewn together and stuffed. An old charm to ward off nasty people is to stuff a poppet with stinging nettles and thorns. This spell rests on a similar principle, although the object of the working is to fend off the unpleasantness of hardship rather than unpleasant people.

 HOW TO CAST THE SPELL

YOU WILL NEED

One black candle, 6–8"/15–20 cm in length

Matches or a lighter

One charcoal disk in a fireproof dish

Two pieces of cloth cut identically into a humanoid shape approximately 6"/15 cm high

One sewing needle

One 36"/90 cm length of black cotton thread

One large bundle of dried dandelions

One large bundle of dried thyme

Three finely chopped thistle heads

TIMING Work on a waning moon to dispel negativity and deflect hardship.

CASTING THE SPELL

1 Cast a circle in accordance with the guidelines on pages 32–36.

2 Light the charcoal, then the candle. Place a little of each herb onto the charcoal.

3 Sew the two pieces of cloth together around the edges, leaving the head edges open, chanting the following:

Guard my wealth and guard my weal
None to envy, none to steal.

The herbs used here are known for their properties to attract good fortune and fend off bad. Dandelions are particularly lucky and attract good friends for bad times. Thistles are highly protective, and thyme is renowned for its ability to repel negativity. All of these should be collected in the wild and dried naturally prior to the spell casting.

It doesn't matter where you keep this poppet, as long as it never leaves your home or is found by one who envies you. Should either event occur, cast the spell again as soon as possible, as all the good you have achieved will have been undone.

Stuff the legs with dandelion, saying:
Walk in the way of fortune.
Stuff the rest of the body with thyme, saying:
Protect all I need.

Now stuff the head with the thistle heads, saying:
*Guard against wrath
Avarice and greed.*

4 Sew up the head; then embroider eyes and a mouth.

5 Hold the poppet over the incense smoke, and show it to the candle flame, saying:
Bend to no will but mine.

6 Keep the poppet safely in your home, and guard it from envious eyes.

HEARTH SPELL
TO BLESS YOUR HOME

PURPOSE Use this spell to bless your home and all who live in it.

BACKGROUND It is such a natural thing to wish to bless your home with good fortune that we are spoiled with choices when selecting a spell to do the job—there are simply hundreds of them! This spell fits the bill, however, and has been included for its simplicity and beauty. But why a Hearth Spell? Because the hearth has been considered since ancient times the heart of the home. The Celtic fire goddess, Brigid, is called on here to bless your home, and the symbol constructed in the course of the spell work is sometimes referred to as Brigid's Cross.

HOW TO CAST THE SPELL

YOU WILL NEED

One charcoal disk in a fireproof dish

One red candle, 6–8"/15–20 cm in length

Matches or a lighter

One teaspoon of benzoin gum

Twelve straight twigs approximately 6"/15 cm in length

One spool of natural twine

One pinch of cinnamon

TIMING Cast on a waxing moon to draw blessings forth, with Sunday or Monday—sun and moon days—being particularly favorable.

CASTING THE SPELL

1 Cast a circle in accordance with the guidelines on pages 32–35.

2 Light the charcoal and the candle, saying:
Holy Brigid of the sacred flame,
Bless the charm I make in your name.
Place a little benzoin on the charcoal.

3 Using the twigs and twine, divide the twigs into four groups of three. Fasten them together so that a 2"/5 cm square is formed at the center. This involves placing the end of one bunch of three at right angles to another bunch, 2"/5 cm from the end of the first bunch.

When all homes had open fires, the hearth formed the focal point for cooking, drying, warmth, light, and company. Nowadays, in older houses, gas or electric heaters may have replaced the open grate of a coal, peat, or wood fire; in this case, your hearth is probably where it always was. If your home was built with central heating and without open fire grates, you will have to decide where the focal point of your home is. Think about a spot where everyone gathers and that, intuitively, you feel is the heart of the home. This is the place where you should hang your charm.

4 Repeat this around the square so that a cross is formed with a square as its center. Bind the twine around the bottom of the twigs to secure them.

5 Place more benzoin and the cinnamon onto the charcoal, and cense the *Bridiog*, or Brigid's cross, in the smoke, saying:
I call upon the four winds
To breathe lightly on this house,
I call upon Brigid's blessing.

6 Hang the Brigid's Cross over the hearth.

BAY CRADLE CHARM
TO BLESS AND PROTECT
A NEWBORN BABY

PURPOSE To bring blessings to a new baby.

BACKGROUND The leaves of the sweet bay, or *Laurus nobilis*, are well known for their culinary uses, but, magically, bay is used for its protective and positive properties. It is often used in vision-inducing incenses, carried as an amulet, or placed in sachets for healing and protection. Occasionally it is scattered on the floor in circles where negativity is being combated.

In this spell, it is used for protection, but mainly for its many blessings. Its virtues in dispelling evil thoughts and intents are legendary, and its wholesome nature makes it a particularly good herb to use to protect and bless a newborn. One of the properties of bay is that it invokes the energies of its planetary ruler—the sun—and all the associated blessings of health, success, prosperity, and joy. In magical terms, bay is synonymous with success, recognition, achievement, and realizing your potential for goodness. All deities associated with this plant represent growth and prosperity, reflecting bay's favorable aspects.

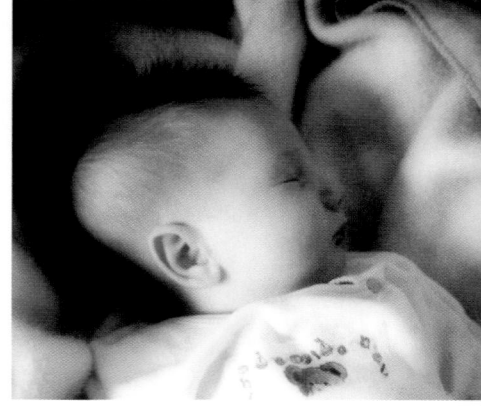

Ensure, for safety, that this sachet is properly secured under a crib mattress. It is not intended for an infant beyond six weeks old.

324

HOW TO CAST THE SPELL

TIMING Work on a waxing moon to bring blessings, and on a Sunday, sacred to the sun gods and goddesses linked with bay.

CASTING THE SPELL

1 Cast a circle in accordance with the guidelines on pages 32–35.

2 Sew three red Xs in a circular position at one end of the strip of cheesecloth.

3 Fold the cheesecloth in half with the Xs on the inside, and sew up two seams; then turn it right side outward.

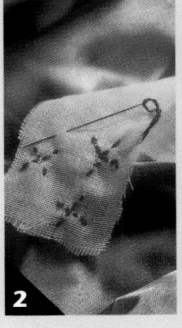

4 Light the candle, saying:

Lamp of the sun
Show your face
To this child
Warm [his/her] life
With your joy.

5 Place the bay leaves one by one into the sachet, saying:

One to shine upon your face
Two to keep you in good grace
Three to make your heart to sing
Four good fortune so to bring
Five for strength in any danger
Six for kindness from a stranger
Seven for good wisdom's crown
Eight for gathering high renown
Nine by which this spell is bound.

YOU WILL NEED

One 4" x 2"/10 cm x 5 cm strip of cheesecloth

One embroidery needle

One skein of red embroidery silk

One gold or orange candle, 6–8"/15–20 cm in length

Matches or a lighter

Nine bay leaves

6 Sew up the remaining side, and attach it to the baby's cradle.

RING OF ROSES SPELL
TO BLESS AND PROTECT A COUPLE AND THEIR RELATIONSHIP

PURPOSE   To bless and protect a couple and their relationship. You can perform this charm for yourself or to offer to newlyweds, or to a couple setting up home together.

BACKGROUND   It can be hard work keeping a relationship going once the early days of romance fade into everyday reality. This spell is for keeping a relationship strong and magically blessing it with endurance. It could be that you have friends who are truly inspirational in their devotion to each other, and you wish to mark your appreciation of what their warm and stable relationship means to those around them. In that case, this is a lovely gift, as it dries to an attractive appearance.

Roses are the archetypal symbol of love—especially red, pink, and white ones. Yellow roses, according to the lexicon of flowers and love, are for platonic friendship only and should not be offered to lovers, as they have the reputation of sending the wrong message! Red roses symbolize love and passion, while pink roses speak of loving affection and a true liking and admiration for a partner. White roses represent love in a pure form and show that your feelings are open, honest, and unselfish.

Needless to say, this spell favors red, pink, and white roses, with the last representing the kind of friendship that true love offers.

HOW TO CAST THE SPELL

TIMING Cast this spell on a waxing moon to bring blessings, and on a Friday, sacred to Venus, the love planet.

CASTING THE SPELL

1 Cast a circle in accordance with the guidelines on pages 32–35.

2 Light the red candle, saying:
Bind it with passion.

3 Light the pink candle, saying:
Bind it with kindness
Light the white candle, saying:
Bind it with light.

4 Using the florist wire and interspersing the colors, fasten the roses into a ring, securing each rose approximately 1"/2.5 cm below the flower head to 1"/2.5 cm below the flower of the rose before. Use the remaining lengths of stem to strengthen the ring, fastening them with the wire and covering them with tape.

5 When the ring is complete, wind twine clockwise around it between the rose heads, chanting:
As I wind this circle round
Love and blessings shall be found.

YOU WILL NEED

One red, one pink, and one white candle, all 6-8"/15–20 cm in length

Matches or a lighter

Six each of red, pink, and white roses

One reel of green florist wire

One reel of green florist tape

One spool of natural twine

6 The ring should be hung in the couple's bedroom.

WAYFARER SPELL
A BLESSING SPELL FOR TRAVELERS

PURPOSE To bring blessings to those about to set out on their travels.

BACKGROUND One famous Irish blessing begins: "May the road rise up to meet you." This is a poetic way of wishing the traveler a pleasant journey free of the usual hardships to be met on the road. This spell has a similar intention, as it is designed to attract all of the blessings that make traveling a worthwhile, safe, and interesting experience. The needs of even the most weathered traveler include the basics that most people require in their own homes: shelter, warmth, food, health, good company, and a little luck. This spell is directed toward ensuring that these are granted.

   This spell calls on the powers of three goddesses associated with the open road and invokes their abilities to steer travelers in the right direction. Annis, a goddess beloved of the traveling peoples of Britain and Europe, is a good friend of travelers who wander from well-trodden paths. Helen, a Welsh deity, is a goddess of crossroads and for those who have directions to choose from, while Cardea, a Roman goddess of gateways, opens the way to learning experiences and wisdom.

HOW TO CAST THE SPELL

YOU WILL NEED

One tea-light in a jar

Matches or a lighter

One pouch containing a mixture of the following:

One tablespoon of ash from a home fire or bonfire at your home

One tablespoon of dried hyssop

Three teaspoons each of dried mint, sugar, and breadcrumbs

Three leaves of fresh basil

TIMING Cast this spell outside on a waxing moon, on the evening before you travel.

CASTING THE SPELL

1 Visualize a white circle of light surrounding you to a distance of approximately 12 feet/3.6 meters.

2 Light the tea-light, saying:
Goddess of travelers, hear me
Lady of the crossroads, hear me
Bright one at the gateway, hear me.

3 Turn to the east, and cast some mixture in that direction, saying:
Spirits of air, grant me easy passage.
Repeat in the south, saying:

Spirits of fire, grant me fireside
companions.
Face west, and repeat, saying:
Spirits of water, grant me the good
opinion of
Those I meet.
Cast the remainder to the north, saying:
Spirits of the earth, grant me food,
shelter, and protection.

4 Standing in the center and facing the direction in which your journey will take you, call out:
Annis, Cardea, Helen of the ways
Hold me safe leaving and returning
Shower your blessings upon me
As the rain refreshes the earth I
walk upon.

SHIELD SPELL
FOR PROTECTION IN STRESSFUL SITUATIONS

PURPOSE To ward off stress.

BACKGROUND It is now generally recognized that an overload of stress is very bad for our physical and mental health. One effect of being placed in stressful situations too often is that our physical and psychological responses make us less able to cope with problems with which we are presented. Adrenaline helps us flee from danger, but it undermines our thought processes when our habitual response, when faced with pressure or the unexpected, is to panic. This spell wields protection from excess stress both generally and in given situations.

HOW TO CAST THE SPELL

YOU WILL NEED

One black candle, 6–8"/15–20 cm in length

Matches or a lighter

One 12"/30 cm length of string

One small, lockable box

TIMING Work on a waning moon to turn anxiety aside, and on Tuesday, day of defensive Mars.

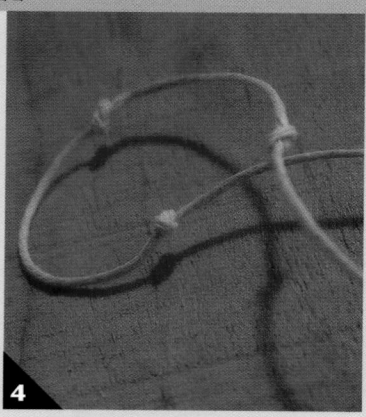

4

Once you have cast this spell, it is easy to summon up its power at exactly the right moment. This does demand concentration and an ability to shut out invasive thoughts, but this in itself is quite good practice for focusing, and for keeping stress at bay.

The image deployed here is that of a wall of shields, an infantry maneuver known as the *testudo* or "tortoise," used by the Roman army to protect forward-moving troops. This spell will protect you as you progress through workaday worries and enable you to continue to move forward positively even when faced with difficulties.

CASTING THE SPELL

1 Cast a circle in accordance with the guidelines on pages 32–35.

2 Light the candle, saying:
Banish my fears.

3 Sit on the floor in the center of the circle, facing north. Close your eyes and slow your breathing, then clear your mind. When you are ready, visualize an oblong shield protecting you from chin to knee. Tie a knot in the string.

4 Now visualize more shields overlapping to cover your sides, back, and head, and tie another knot for each. Relax within your shield "shell," allowing yourself to feel secure and protected.

5 When you are ready, open your eyes, and drip wax from the candle onto each knot you have tied.

6 Lock the knotted string in the box, and keep it in a safe place. Whenever you feel the need to invoke your shield, summon up the image of the testudo covering and defending you.

SALT AND WATER SPELL
A SELF-BLESSING FOR TIMES OF TROUBLE

PURPOSE To use in difficult times, when you need great inner strength.

BACKGROUND When we find ourselves in difficult circumstances that are unlikely to find a simple solution, it may be difficult to remember how strong we really are. Sometimes the situation will require our attention for a long period of time, and it is when we face what seems to be an unending tunnel that we need to provide a little light for ourselves.

This self-blessing should be used only when in need, to preserve its potency. Many witches and magicians recognize that the spiritual value of this type of ritual is made stronger by using it very seldom. The symbolism is very simple: salt represents the shield and protection of earth; the candlelight brings hope and courage; the water brings spiritual transformation and cleansing; and the incense carries our prayer of blessing into the ether, to be relayed into the web of spirit.

Prior to using this blessing, think about a god or goddess with whom you have a strong natural affinity, and call on them by name in this spell to witness your self-blessing. It can be profoundly self-empowering and strengthening to keep a symbol or totem of that deity close to you in times of trouble.

HOW TO CAST THE SPELL

YOU WILL NEED

One charcoal disk in a fireproof dish

One white candle, 6–8"/15–20 cm
in length

Matches or a lighter

One teaspoon of frankincense

One container of salt with a flow hole

One wineglass filled with spring water

TIMING To be cast when in need, rather
than at any particular phase of the moon.

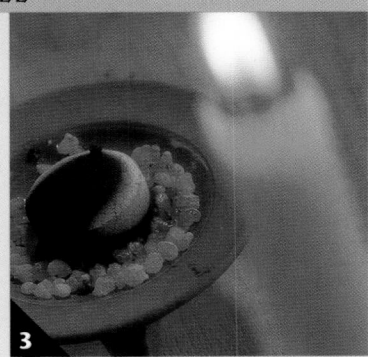

CASTING THE SPELL

1 Cast a circle in accordance with the
guidelines on pages 32–35.

2 Light the charcoal, then the candle,
saying:
   I walk the path of courage
   Where truth brings light.

3 Sprinkle the frankincense onto the
charcoal, and inhale the scent, saying:
   May [God/Goddess name] hear me in
   the darkest night.

4 Pour some salt into your left palm,
and place your right palm over the water,
saying:
   Water, wash away all evil.

Place your right hand over the salt,
and say:
   Salt, cast out impurity.
Add the salt to the water, and anoint your
feet, knees, navel, breast, and forehead
with it.

5 Pour the salt all around you in a
clockwise circle, saying:
   [God/Goddess name], walk with me
   in my footsteps.
Treading on the salt, walk around it
clockwise in a complete circle; then return
to the center.

6 Close your eyes and silently ask to
be blessed with whatever qualities you
feel will carry you through your time
of trouble.

DIVINATION SPELLS

INTRODUCTION TO DIVINATION SPELLS

The annals of magic are replete with
old country customs that lay claim to
the ability to see into the future. Tales
of unmarried women placing wedding
cake beneath their pillows to dream
of a future husband rub shoulders
with rather more morbid theories for
predicting who will die in the next year.
Beneath the superstitions and the
bloodcurdling stories can be found the
skeletal frame of magical traditions.
In this section you will find spells
containing formulas that may seem
faintly familiar, precisely because their
genesis is in the origins of some well-
known customs.

Divination, of course, is not just about
foretelling the future. It is also about
reading patterns that already exist in
order to get a better picture of what is
possible. The majority of tarot card
readers, for example, are not "fortune-
tellers" but experienced readers of the
patterns of the present, symbolized
within the various permutations of the
card spreads. Similarly, palm readers may

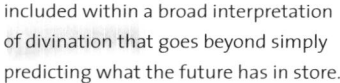

have predictive abilities, but much of their wisdom relies on reading your past and present in patterns set against a system of planetary symbolism. All of the magical recipes in this section are

included within a broad interpretation of divination that goes beyond simply predicting what the future has in store.

The spells in this section are likewise diverse and are ranged around a number of different purposes. Here you will find the means by which to find solutions to problems and to discover who is false and who is true. For the romantic soul, there are traditional spells to discover the identity of your true love, to find out if your affections are returned, and to offer clues as to the nature of a future partner. There are, of course, spells for reading the patterns of what is likely to come.

You should remember, when using any of these spells, that the future is not set in stone—it hasn't happened yet! All that any of these spells can show— in common with any self-styled fortune-teller—are the likely configurations of what is coming. How you respond to that likelihood is what will make your future. Belief in "fate" can be stultifying—and, indeed, the opposite of magic, which is always about change and transformation. A warning: if you keep repeating the same spell in pursuit of the same problem, you will get distorted readings. If you approach these spells with respect and common sense, you will not be disappointed.

BONES AND STONES SPELL
TO CAST ONE'S FUTURE

PURPOSE To give a reading on which to base future choices in your life.

BACKGROUND A custom in South Africa, which appears to be based on very ancient ancestor worship, is the use of bones in divination. The use of a relative's finger bones is thought to invoke the knowledge of those who stand outside the world of the living in order to gain insights into the future. The person reading the bones has a personal set, each of which has different meanings well known to them. The method by which they are read is very simple: they are cast into a marked-out circle, and the pattern in which they fall, and their relationship to each other, offer a message for the soothsayer to divine.

In this spell, you will be combining this old method with that of lithomancy—the practice of reading stones. The stones in question can be obtained from most crystal or rock stores as well as from your surroundings. The "bones" are yarrow stems trimmed to various lengths, as specified on the opposite page.

You will need to use your imagination and your creative and intuitive abilities to read the stones and bones in the combination in which they fall, as each reading is unique. What you divine in your first reading, in a magical circle, is bound to be powerful and meaningful, so if at first you do not understand, try to match the pattern to what is happening in your life at the moment.

HOW TO CAST THE SPELL

TIMING Cast your stones on a dark moon, in accordance with the ancient customs from which this spell originates.

CASTING THE SPELL

Cast a circle in accordance with the guidelines on pages 32–35.

1 Light the black candle to your left and the white candle to your right.

2 With your finger, mark a large circle in the sand with a horizontal line through the center.

3 Shake up the "stones and bones" in your hands, and cast them onto the sand circle.

4 Divine their meaning as follows:

TOP OF THE CIRCLE:	*public life*
BOTTOM OF THE CIRCLE:	*private life*
TO THE LEFT:	*challenges*
TO THE RIGHT:	*the material world*
THE 1"/2.5 CM STEM:	*soon*
THE 2"/5 CM STEM:	*the near future*
THE 3"/7.5 CM STEM:	*the long term*
SHORELINE PEBBLE:	*where problems lie*
CLEAR QUARTZ:	*friends*
ROSE QUARTZ:	*the heart*
AMETHYST:	*skills and career*
CITRINE:	*knowledge*
FLINT:	*beginnings.*

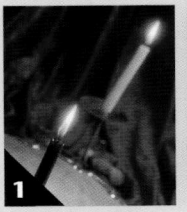

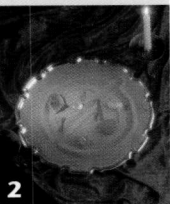

YOU WILL NEED

One white candle, 6–8"/15–20 cm in length

One black candle, 6–8"/15–20 cm in length

Matches or a lighter

One tea tray filled with sand

Three yarrow stems, respectively 1"/2.5 cm, 2"/5 cm, and 3"/7.5 cm in length

One pebble from a shoreline

One tumbled clear quartz

One tumbled rose quartz

One tumbled amethyst

One tumbled citrine

One small sharp flint

MAJOR ARCANA SPELL
TO FIND THE ANSWER TO A QUESTION

PURPOSE To find the answer to a question that is troubling you.

BACKGROUND Tarot cards are consulted for guidance rather than for "yes" or "no" answers, generally speaking, and given the many permutations possible with readings involving seventy-eight cards, advice can indeed be very subtle. Most seasoned tarot readers agree, however, that there are ways in which to work out the timing of events predicted and even means of using the guidance of the cards to offer likely solutions to problems. Some of these methods are generally agreed, whereas others differ between readers. Those who work closely with the

HOW TO CAST THE SPELL

YOU WILL NEED

One purple candle, 6–8"/15–20 cm in length

Matches or a lighter

Twenty-two major arcana tarot cards

TIMING Lay your cards out on a waxing half-moon (sometimes known as the first quarter) to divine all possibilities offered in the spread.

CASTING THE SPELL

Cast a circle in accordance with the guidelines on pages 32–35.

1 Light the purple candle, saying:
Fortuna, goddess of the wheel
Look kindly on my quest for truth.

2 Shuffle the cards, and lay all of them face down in the center of the circle.

3 With your question in mind, pass your writing hand over them, and pick up three that you are drawn to.

4 Lay them face up before you, from left to right, in the order in which you chose them.

tarot often note that when particular cards appear, they always carry a particular message to them, even if this is outside of the usual meaning ascribed to that card in the deck.

This spell rests on principles that are based upon generally agreed tarot wisdom. You should be prepared to do some hard thinking if the answer offered by the cards appears to be more subtle than you had hoped, but be assured that the guidance offered will be genuine if your need is sincere. Accept the first casting and read your answer on the basis of the guidance offered below.

5 The card on the left represents the basis of your problem; the one in the center represents its present effects; and the card on the right represents the outcome.

6 Refer to the following guidelines to features that appear on any of the cards in order to read your answer accurately:

EVEN NUMBER:	truth
ODD NUMBER:	falsehood
MAN:	immediately
WOMAN:	within a year
MAN AND WOMAN:	leave it be
A CUP:	yes
A SWORD:	no
SUN, MOON, OR STAR:	your own judgment is correct
ANIMAL:	justice will be attained
WATER:	movement, travel, change.

PENDULUM SPELL
TO DETECT A LOST OR DESIRED ITEM

PURPOSE To locate a lost item or to locate something you have been looking for.

BACKGROUND Pendulums are ancient divination tools, favored for their simplicity as well as their amazing powers. A more recent use to which they have been put involves maps, where a pendulum is suspended over a two-dimensional representation of an area being searched.

Traditionally, this technique uses one of two methods, the first being that of reaction and the second that of confirmation and negation. The former is based on any reaction at all from the pendulum: if it moves, the location is confirmed. It may also react very strongly over the correct point. The latter, based on a "yes" or "no" response, relies on the direction in which the pendulum rotates. Rotation clockwise denotes "yes," and counterclockwise means "no."

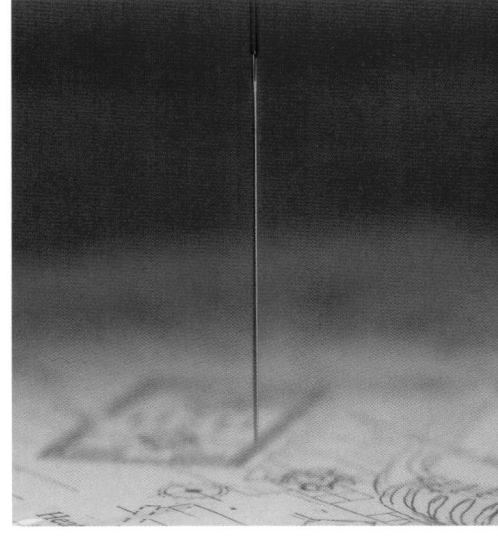

Before casting this circle, you will need to test your pendulum to see how it reacts when you use it. Test it by asking questions to which the answers are obvious, for example— "Is today Monday?"—and see what sort of response you get. This will guide you when it comes to divining the location of your lost or sought-after object.

HOW TO CAST THE SPELL

YOU WILL NEED

One white candle, 6–8"/15–20 cm in length

Matches or a lighter

One black ink pen

One sheet of office paper
or
One map of the search area

One sewing needle

One 24"/60 cm length of black cotton thread

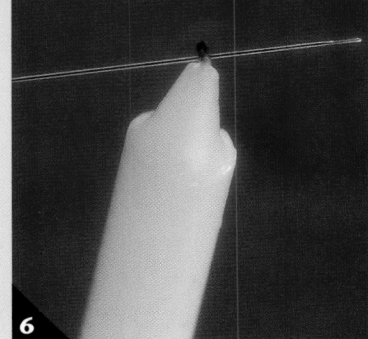

TIMING Test your divination abilities on the dark of the moon.

CASTING THE SPELL

1 Cast a circle in accordance with the guidelines on pages 32–35.

2 Light the candle, saying:
Spirit that aids the traveler and
Guides the birds in their flight
Empower this spell to find [name object]
Guide and help me in my quest
North to south and east to west.

3 Draw a simple map of your home if the object you are seeking lies there, or use the map, as appropriate.

4 Thread the needle, then double the thread over, and fasten it. Suspend the needle over the map, pinching the knot at the end of the thread between the thumb and forefinger of your writing hand.

5 Allow your mind to go blank as you move to different locations on the map to test the response of the pendulum. Be patient, and take as long as you need to judge the response of the pendulum.

6 When you are satisfied with your answer, blow out the candle, and pierce the wick through the molten wax at the top with the needle of the pendulum.

NEEDLE AND CANDLE SPELL
TO UNCOVER A LIAR

PURPOSE To discover deceit in another.

BACKGROUND This magical equivalent of a polygraph test has an interesting pedigree. For hundreds of years, a test for a thief was to place needles in the side of a candle and seat all the suspects around it. As the candle burned down, the needles would fall, and the first to fall would be denounced as a thief. This spell is more of a lie detector than a thief catcher, but the principle is very much the same. Before putting this spell to the test, however, you should ask yourself some hard questions. First of all,

HOW TO CAST THE SPELL

YOU WILL NEED

One white candle, 6–8"/15–20 cm in length

Matches or a lighter

One sheet of office paper

One pen with green ink

One beeswax candle, 6–8"/15–20 cm in length

Seven sewing needles

TIMING Cast this spell at the full moon.

CASTING THE SPELL

1 Cast a circle in accordance with the guidelines on pages 32–35.

2 Light the white candle, saying:
   Shadows take flight
   In the moon's light.

3 Turn the paper so that its longest side is horizontal, and draw a vertical line straight through the middle of it. On one half of the paper, draw the outline of seven swords, pointing inward. On the other half, draw a circle with a dot in the center. Place the beeswax candle in a secure holder on the center of the paper.

ask yourself whether you are right to suspect deceit or simply being paranoid or unreasonable. If you are being foolish, you will simply get a skewed answer from this test. Secondly, ask whether by casting this spell you are simply opting out of a much-needed confrontation. If you are, the person who is deceiving you will continue to believe that you are soft enough to fall for the same tricks again.

If you can answer the above questions to your own satisfaction, press on with the spell, which should help you to judge who is lying and who is telling the truth.

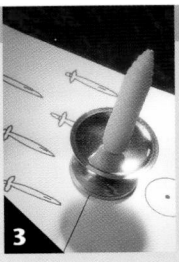

4 Heat the points of the needles and place them at equal distances and at the same level into the beeswax, about 1"/2.5 cm below the wick, so that they stick out from it horizontally.

5 Light the candle, saying:
The seven swords
Shall judge thy words.
While you are waiting for the candle to burn down to the needles, chant the following words:
Will know you
When you fall.

6 If the first needle to fall comes down on the side of the swords, you are being deceived; if it comes down on the side of the circle and dot, you are deceiving yourself.

DAISY SPELL
TO DISCOVER YOUR LIFE'S TASK

PURPOSE   To help you to find your purpose in life.

BACKGROUND   One of the most important questions we ever ask ourselves is why we are here and what our task is in this life. This goes beyond searching for a career path, a partner, or surroundings in which we feel settled—it goes right to the heart of finding purpose in our existence. Whatever your religious or spiritual beliefs, it is possible to ask this question in order to seek self-knowledge and to search for your place and purpose in the world. The final answer will come with experience and revelation, but setting off on this path of discovery without any idea of direction can be daunting. This spell will help you to find your way.

You will need to cast this spell when daisies are in season, as they are its main ingredient. Daisies have long been used for divination purposes. Children are often seen tearing the petals off one by one, chanting, "She loves me, she loves me not." Sometimes they are used in very much the same way as cherry stones, to find out what your future status in life is likely to be. Here they are used to offer you clues as to the gift that you bring to others in your lifetime.

HOW TO CAST THE SPELL

YOU WILL NEED

One stick of sandalwood incense in a holder

One white candle, 6–8"/15–20 cm in length

Matches or a lighter

One sewing needle

Seven daisies, freshly picked

TIMING This spell is best cast on the night of the full moon.

CASTING THE SPELL

1 Cast a circle in accordance with the guidelines on pages 32–35.

2 Light the incense, then the candle.

3 Using the needle, make a daisy chain by piercing a hole near the end of six of them and threading them together in a ring.

4 Holding the remaining daisy in your left hand, remove the petals one by one, chanting the following lines in order of their removal:

MAKER

SHAKER

CARER

SHARER

HEALER

5 The word on which the last petal is shed indicates which gifts you have to offer others:

MAKER: you have the gift of creating things of great practical use or beauty.

SHAKER: you have the ability to get things changed by word and action.

CARER: your strength lies in supporting others.

SHARER: you are a negotiator, a peacemaker, and one who achieves justice and fairness.

HEALER: you have the gift of healing.

6 Place the daisy chain under your pillow, as dreams over the next seven nights will offer further clues to your life's task.

FETCH SPELL
TO DISCOVER IF THE PERSON YOU DESIRE RETURNS YOUR FEELINGS

PURPOSE To find out whether the object of your affections has feelings for you.

BACKGROUND The tradition of the fetch has a number of different stories attached to it. In the Irish tradition, a *fetch* is a likeness of a person seen before their death, while Nordic traditions see a fetch as something akin to a totem, or personal power animal. English customs understand fetch to mean a likeness that is sent by a living person to take a message to a specified individual.

In this spell, you will send your fetch to put the person you desire in mind of you and to establish whether or not they return your interest. In terms of sending a likeness of yourself to visit someone, this spell is similar to the Magic Mirror Spell on pages 56–57, which is designed to help you send a comfort or reminder to a lover. This spell, however, is intended to draw out a reaction from the person to whom you are sending your fetch, and the methodology is somewhat different.

There is a magical "health warning" attached to this spell: if your intended is not interested, do not continue to send your fetch, as you will find yourself drained of energy. This is not because the magic employed involves a dangerous amount of effort but because obsession itself can exact a toll all its own, and magic will simply amplify this process.

HOW TO CAST THE SPELL

TIMING The best time to send out your fetch is on a full moon.

CASTING THE SPELL

1 Cast a circle in accordance with the guidelines on pages 32–35.

2 Light the charcoal, then the candle, saying:

I call upon she who is queen of
All witcheries
To lend me her power
Hail, triple Hecate.

3 Mix the orris root, bay leaves, and mugwort in the mortar with the pestle until it is thoroughly mixed, and sprinkle it onto the charcoal.

YOU WILL NEED

One charcoal disk in a fireproof dish

One silver or gray candle, 6–8"/15–20 cm in length

Matches or a lighter

One pinch of powdered orris root

One teaspoon of dried bay leaves

One pinch of mugwort

Mortar and pestle

4 Sitting in the center of the circle and facing north, close your eyes, and slow your breathing. Imagine stepping out of your body, getting up from the floor, and turning to face yourself. Keeping the image of the standing figure, return to your perspective in the seated position.

5 Allow the figure before you to turn and face you, and when it does, tell it where it should go and to whom it should appear. Add that it has only one month's life and that after that it will dissolve.

6 If the desired one returns your interest, they will approach you within forty days.

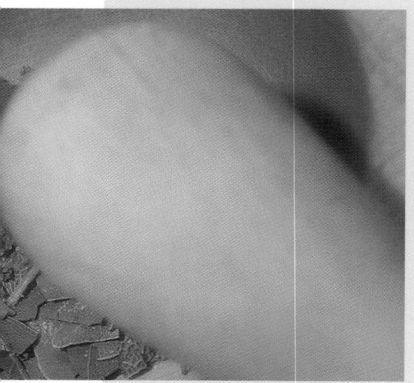

TEA LEAF SPELL
TO READ FORTUNES

PURPOSE To help identify where your fortune lies.

BACKGROUND The art of tea leaf reading, or tasseography, is thought to be thousands of years old and possibly originated in China. It is a psychic art, with guidelines rather than hard-and-fast rules. Individual tea leaf readers build a vocabulary of meanings that match the patterns formed during a reading; their methods are refined through experience rather than through rote learning of the shapes and correspondences. Happily for beginners, however, there are a few simple guidelines to help you get started.

This spell is undertaken to find out and identify where your fortune will be taking you in the next year, so you should not perform this spell for yourself again until at least another thirteen moon cycles have passed. If, following this spell, you wish to develop your skills in reading the tea leaves, you should practice this outside of the circle and try it on willing friends.

If you wish to ask specific questions for yourself within a year of casting this spell, they should be very focussed and not a general fortune reading, as you will get distorted readings and break faith with your own developing skills.

HOW TO CAST THE SPELL

YOU WILL NEED

One purple candle, 6–8"/15–20 cm in length

Matches or a lighter

One teapot containing a teaspoon of loose tea leaves and a cupful of boiling water

One teacup and saucer

TIMING This spell, to seek your fortune in the coming year, is best cast on a waxing or full moon. Readings outside of the circle can take place on any phase of the moon.

CASTING THE SPELL

1 Cast a circle in accordance with the guidelines on pages 32–35.

2 Light the candle, saying:

Spirit of fortune
Guide me and show
The line of my fortune
And all I must know.

3 Pour unstrained tea into the cup.

4 Sip it until one teaspoon of tea remains in the bottom.

5 Swirl the leaves around thirteen times; then turn the cup over onto the saucer.

6 Read the residue of leaves as follows, from these very general guidelines:

LEAVES NEAR THE RIM OF THE CUP:	*events coming soon*
LEAVES AROUND THE SIDE:	*events in the near future*
LEAVES IN THE BOTTOM OF THE CUP:	*in the long term*
HORSESHOE:	*good fortune, travel, a wedding*
BALL:	*there will be ups and downs*
CIRCLE:	*life has surprises in store*
ARROW:	*news coming soon*
DISKS:	*money coming in*
BASKET OR BAG:	*a baby*
NEAR THE HANDLE:	*traps and deceit*
ELSEWHERE:	*money coming in*
ANIMALS:	*be on your guard*
LINES:	*worries*
SQUARES:	*security.*

CONFETTI SPELL
TO DISCOVER THE IDENTITY OF YOUR FUTURE PARTNER

PURPOSE   To help singles to discover the identity of a future partner.

BACKGROUND   There must be thousands of customs and traditions that claim to reveal the identity of your future life partner. This in itself indicates how important we consider committed relationships in our lives. If you are single, looking for a serious romance, and ready to find the right person long term, then this spell is for you.

In sympathetic magic, "like represents like," as they say. But like also begets like, which is why so many superstitions referring to finding a partner are linked to weddings. This spell requires you to collect the main ingredient for it—confetti—from a wedding that has just taken place. This means some detective work and a little skulking around, and it may also depend on the inefficiency of cleaning services at the local church, registry office, or town hall!

It is best to take a bag with you, so that you can scoop up a good quantity of the confetti deposited by a wedding party as the bride and groom leave the ceremony.

HOW TO CAST THE SPELL

YOU WILL NEED

One white candle, 6–8"/15–20 cm in length

Matches or a lighter

One large bag of confetti, collected after a wedding ceremony

TIMING Work when the first visible crescent after the dark moon can actually be seen in the sky.

CASTING THE SPELL

1 Cast a circle in accordance with the guidelines on pages 32–35.

2 Light the white candle in the east of the circle, saying:

Bright morning star rising
And shining above
Shine down on this circle
Reveal my true love.

3 Stand in the middle of the circle, and bow to the north. Then face east, closing your eyes, and shower all of the confetti onto your head.

4 Keep your eyes closed and count to thirteen, then open them.

5 Examine the patterns of the confetti as it has fallen around you, and judge the likely identity of your future partner from these guidelines:

AN EVEN CIRCLE AROUND YOU
It is someone you know.

SMALL PILES
It will be somebody who is good with money.

STRAIGHT LINES
Look out for an honest stranger.

ARCS AND SMALL CIRCLES
It will be someone gentle and kind.

ANGLES AND SQUARES
You will marry somebody tall and serious.

UNEVEN DISTRIBUTION
It will be somebody exciting and sensual.

NO DISCERNIBLE PATTERNS
You will meet in unusual circumstances.

MORE BEHIND THAN BEFORE YOU
It will be somebody older than you.

MORE BEFORE THAN BEHIND YOU
Your happiness will be long-lived.

GRAVEYARD DUST SPELL
TO UNCOVER AN ENEMY

PURPOSE To provide a way of discovering one who wishes you ill.

BACKGROUND The origins of this spell are lost in the mists of time, but different versions of it emerge from time to time as ways of discovering evildoers or secret enemies. The main intent of this spell is to uncover one who is acting against your interests while playing the friend; it works best either if you already have your

suspicions about someone, or if the person upsetting you has been approaching your home. This may sound rather odd, but the behavior of people who set out to deceive very often *is* odd. Sometimes they might do upsetting things, such as post poison-pen letters by hand, or alert you by asking strange questions or being around at times you do not expect them to be. That said, if you do suspect someone is playing you false, set your trap for a time when you know they will be coming to your home. Otherwise, leave their coming to chance.

Needless to say, if you suspect dangerous or compulsive behavior, you should get help and advice immediately; but if you wish to uncover an enemy yourself, then this ancient spell may help stop them in their tracks—literally.

HOW TO CAST THE SPELL

TIMING Carry out the first part of this spell on the night of the dark moon, and thereafter at dusk on the next day.

CASTING THE SPELL

1 Cast a circle in accordance with the guidelines on pages 32–35.

2 Light the black candle, saying:
By the skull of the moon
Mine enemy be shown.

3 Pour the ash cinders into the bowl, and place both hands palm down upon it, saying:
Betwixt these hands
All safe and sound
Below them the path of
Truth.

4 Spread the ash on your front walk or driveway. At dusk the next evening, go out to see if the footprint of the suspected enemy is on the ground, or if an unknown foot has trodden near your home.

5 Using the knife, draw a circle in the ground around it. Drive a nail into the footprint, saying:
Fare as fair as you would merit
Merit as fair as you would fare.

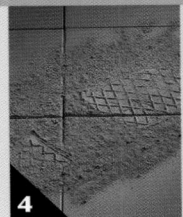
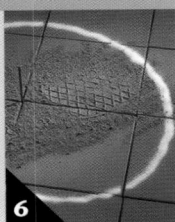

YOU WILL NEED

One black candle, 6–8"/15–20 cm in length

Matches or a lighter

Ash from an ash (wood) fire, 1 lb/450 g

One bowl

One black-handled knife

One hammer and nail

One container of salt with a flow hole

6 Pour a circle of salt around the footprint. Within a moon, the enemy will betray themselves.

ACORN SPELL
TO PREDICT IF YOU WILL MARRY OR MEET YOUR LIFETIME PARTNER WITHIN A YEAR

PURPOSE To help singles find out if they are likely to meet their lifetime partner within the next twelve months.

BACKGROUND This is a delightful spell to share with friends, if they are willing. It is ideal for a bridal or groom shower—especially if there are a number of singles at the party—or even for a New Year's celebration. The idea of this spell is to predict whether you will marry or meet your lifetime partner in the course of the coming year. Although it is a fun

spell, it also has its serious side; if you call on magic to predict, then you should respect what it has to say and not cast this more than once in a twelve-month period.

This spell is based on a very old custom regarding trees. Many trees in ancient cultures were considered sacred. Oak trees are still held in great reverence in parts of England and Ireland and symbolize, among other things, truth and steadfastness. Acorns, the seeds of these mighty trees, sprout inside cups that at one time were thought to be the drinking vessels of fairies. In particular, the cups represent sacred potential, for they bear and carry a small seed that grows into a gigantic tree. To use acorn cups in a spell to divine future happiness is to use a potent and magical ingredient, for as the country folk say: "From little acorns there do grow mighty oaks!"

HOW TO CAST THE SPELL

YOU WILL NEED

One acorn cup for each person

One indelible soft-tip pen

One green candle, 6–8"/15–20 cm in length

Matches or a lighter

One large bowl

One long-handled wooden spoon

TIMING Cast this spell at any phase of the moon and on any day of the week—but cast it only once a year.

CASTING THE SPELL

1 Get everyone involved to write their initials with the indelible ink pen on the inside of their acorn cup.

2 Light the green candle, and get everyone involved to repeat the following words when it is lit:

Mighty oak
Greenwood tree
When is
Happiness to be?

3 Take the wooden spoon, and stir the waters three times clockwise, three times counterclockwise, and then once clockwise, in quick succession.

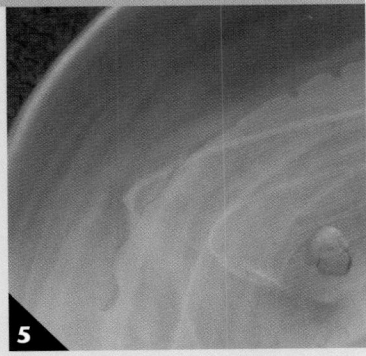

4 Get the first candidate to drop in their acorn cup, and count to seven.

5 If the acorn cup touches the side of the bowl within that time, they will marry or meet their lifetime partner in the course of the next year.

ANCIENT KNOT SPELL
TO FIND A SOLUTION TO A PROBLEM

PURPOSE To bring inspiration to those seeking to find the answer to a tricky problem.

BACKGROUND To those facing a predicament and struggling to find the best way to deal with it, the notion that a spell can help may seem ridiculous. However, when a decision requiring both imagination and common sense is required—and soon—it is often the case that what is lacking is inspiration. Much of the time we subconsciously know the solution to problems in our lives, even if we are consciously avoiding it. Unlocking that knowledge is the object of this spell, which is based on a very old charm.

 HOW TO CAST THE SPELL

YOU WILL NEED

One charcoal disk in a fireproof dish

One pale blue candle, 6–8"/15–20 cm in length

Matches or a lighter

One teaspoon of wormwood (*Artemisia absinthium*)

One 9"/22.5 cm length of string

TIMING This spell should be cast at any phase after the full moon until the day after the dark moon.

CASTING THE SPELL

1 Cast a circle in accordance with the guidelines on pages 32–35.

2 Light the incense, then the candle, saying:

You who know the secret
Of the unhewn stone
Whose light shines
In darkness
Light my way.

3 Sprinkle the wormwood onto the charcoal.

In the West, we often use the language of struggle and capture when we speak of dilemmas. We speak of "wrestling" with a problem, being "in" a quandary, or "tied up" in difficulties. Complex issues are spoken of as "knotty"—in line with the notion that we are constrained, held back, or even held captive when beset by them. This spell uses the age-old magical device of tying knots in order to help unravel a tangle. Keep a dream diary for seven days following the casting of this spell to find clues to the answer, looking out for puns and symbols, and trust your wise self to show the way forward.

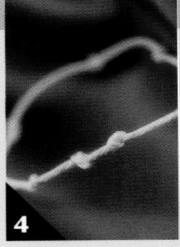

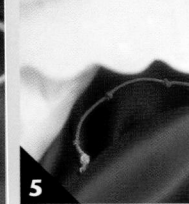

4 Tie seven knots into the string, reciting a line of the following for each one, in the order indicated:

One for the sun who brings the light
Two for the stars that shine at night
Three for the moon who sails the sky
Four for the clouds that pass her by
Five for the babe that's in the moon
Six for the question on my tongue
Seven for secrets yet unknown
Within a se'night all undone.

5 Place the knotted string under your pillow for the next seven nights, undoing one knot each night before you go to sleep.

6 The answer to your problem will come to you in your dreams.

APPLE SPELL
TO DREAM OF YOUR TRUE LOVE

PURPOSE To reveal the identity of your true love in a dream.

BACKGROUND Apples and love go together like a hand in a glove. As well as being the fruit of the Celtic otherworld, apples are closely linked with the element of water, the magical domain of feelings, emotions—and dreams. They are often mentioned in world myths, usually epitomizing that which we most desire. Here, the apple represents news of your future love, and both peel and flesh are featured in the spell.

One of the first spells I ever learned as a child was an old English charm that used apple peel as a way of finding out the name of your future husband. It was specifically

 ### HOW TO CAST THE SPELL

YOU WILL NEED

One charcoal disk in a fireproof dish

One red candle, 6–8"/15–20 cm in length

Matches or a lighter

One teaspoon equal parts orris root and dill

One fresh rosy apple

One sharp black-handled knife

One portable mirror at least 6"/15 cm square

One 3"/7.5 cm square drawstring cheesecloth pouch

TIMING Cast this spell on the night of the full moon.

CASTING THE SPELL

1 Cast a circle in accordance with the guidelines on pages 32–35.

2 Light the charcoal, then the candle, saying:

Goddess of love
True may you prove
Show me [his/her] face
By your good grace.

Sprinkle the incense onto the charcoal.

for girls and women, and it involved peeling an apple, keeping the peel intact, and throwing it over your shoulder to reveal the first letter of your true love's name. A variation of this was to do it at midnight in front of a mirror, and not only would you know his initial, but you would see his face in the mirror. A friend and I tried this, but she went first and was so spooked by the experience that we abandoned the experiment and never did it again!

Although this spell does involve an unbroken apple peel, your true love is reflected in your dreams, rather than in a physical mirror.

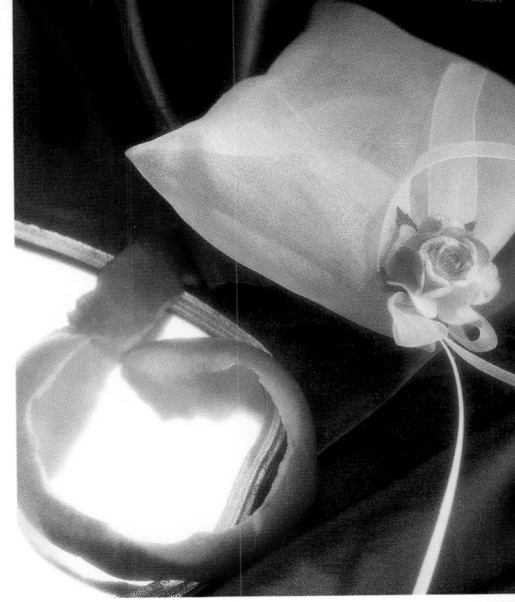

5 Eat the apple. Looking into the mirror, say:

I have eaten knowledge
But not the skin
The skin is returned
When the secret is learned.

6 Place the peel in the pouch, and hang it above your bed until you dream of your true love. The next day, bury the peel in the earth.

3 Peel the apple thinly over the mirror, without breaking the peel.

4 Allow the peel to fall on the mirror. Lifting the mirror, pass it three times in a clockwise circle through the incense smoke.

BANISHING AND BINDING SPELLS

INTRODUCTION TO BANISHING AND BINDING SPELLS

When magicians are approached for help when someone is behaving badly, there is an expectation, and sometimes a fear, that stopping the person necessarily means inflicting harm. These concerns are directly related to the belief that spells that prevent this behavior are hexes or curses intended to harm or damage. Nothing could be farther from the truth; spells that stop bullies, oppressors, and tormentors are designed to prevent harm—not inflict it! The terms *banishing* and *binding* bear this out. To *banish* may mean either to move someone on to another place or to banish an aspect of their behavior that is proving a problem to their peers, neighbors, or co-workers. *To bind someone* is to inhibit their ability to cause damage to others.

Banishing spells work on several levels; they can serve to shift a person away from the context in which they are doing harm, as in the Seat of Thorns Spell in this section, or they can work toward diminishing their power, as in the Cord

and Candle Spell. There is another sense in which banishment is used in magic, and that is to diminish the worst of the damage left in the wake of destructive behavior, as seen in the Ink Wash Spell. This is extended to include emotional detritus left following sad or traumatic

events; here the Severing Spell is designed to help break with the past. Banishing spells can help banish your own bad habits if, with a little imagination, you adapt some of those in the following section. As you can see, there is a lot of scope for addressing harm in the range of banishing spells offered here—and not a curse in sight!

Binding spells are particularly persuasive when used to force someone to acknowledge the consequences of their actions. The Circle of Salt Spell in this section imprisons an evildoer by their own behavior, which will continue to bounce back to them until they decide to behave decently. The Bird's Nest Spell continues this theme, this time providing a more in-your-face, confrontational method, which means that the culprit will find the outcomes of their actions returning to their own doorstep. This type of confrontation offers the chance to the perpetrator to "make good." If they choose not to, then the consequences of their conduct will continue to bedevil them until they cease. Sometimes bindings depend on making visible to others the deceitful deeds of a wrongdoer—and here the powerful Water Elemental Spell provides the means by which to do this.

CIRCLE OF SALT SPELL
TO BIND A WRONGDOER
BY THEIR OWN ACTIONS

PURPOSE To prevent a malefactor from continuing to work harm to others.

BACKGROUND When somebody's bad behavior impacts detrimentally on others, and understanding, persuasion, and even confrontation have not worked, it is time for magic to step in. This spell is a classical binding spell and works on the basis of psychic confinement. To place a representation of the troublemaker within a binding circle of salt is to surround them with a barrier that protects others, while confining the effects of any behavior to the immediate vicinity of its originator. In short, the "harm" created

HOW TO CAST THE SPELL

YOU WILL NEED

One black candle, 6–8"/15–20 cm in length

Matches or a lighter

Strands of hair from the wrongdoer

One 4"/10 cm length of black woolen thread

One circular mirror at least 4"/10 cm in diameter

One container of salt with a flow hole

An open fire in a grate, a brazier, or a bonfire outside

TIMING This spell can be cast at any time, according to need, but it is most powerful if cast on a dark moon, the best time to construct psychic barriers.

CASTING THE SPELL

1 Cast a circle in accordance with the guidelines on pages 32–35.

2 Light the candle, saying:
Dark of moon
All powers surround
Bless this space as sacred ground
Ill confine and harm confound
As I walk this circle round.

will not get out to damage others but land right back at the feet of its creator. This can be enormously useful not only to those who have hitherto suffered from the wrongdoer's behavior, but to the perpetrator themselves; confronted by their behavior, they have a chance to change it.

In magic, salt is a purifying substance and is often mixed with water and sprinkled around a ritual space to psychically clear it before a ritual. Salt also represents the wholesome and defensive nature of this element and here provides a shield against harm.

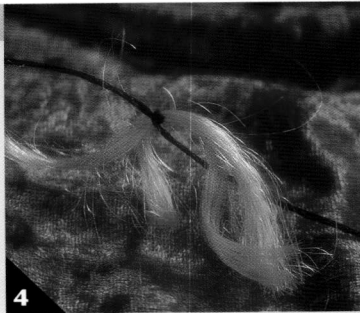

3 Walk the circle in a counterclockwise direction, carrying the candle with you. Return to the center, and set the candle down.

4 Tie the strands of hair in a tight knot using the black wool, saying:
   *[Name of wrongdoer], by my actions
      yours are bound.*

5 Place the hair in the center of the mirror, and pour a circle of salt around it, saying:
   As I make this circle round.

6 Breathe onto the mirror, and throw the hair and salt into the fire, saying:
   *Evil's death
   By my breath.*

CORD AND CANDLE SPELL
TO DIMINISH THE POWER
OF A DECEITFUL PERSON

PURPOSE To take away the power of another to deceive.

BACKGROUND When the burden of proof is not in your favor, but you know that another person is being deceitful to friends, colleagues, or to yourself, this spell is absolutely ideal. Like many other magical workings in this book, the built-in philosophy is to reflect the deeds of the person on whom the spell is focused. If you are wrong or have got the wrong person, then there is nothing to fear in using this on an innocent one. If they are blameless, their honesty will shine through. If not, however, their ability

to deceive will be diminished, and their plans will begin to backfire.

It is important that you place the candleholder securely in a dish, as once the candle burns down, the flame will consume the cord and paper tied around it. Needless to say, all candles allowed to burn down should be properly supervised at all times, but this spell requires a little more care as the cord and paper may fall burning from the candle once it ignites. The paper, which should bear the signature or photocopy of the signature of the person you believe is being dishonest, should be cut down to the minimum size possible without compromising the signature itself.

HOW TO CAST THE SPELL

TIMING This spell can be used at any time, if your need is urgent, but the most favorable time is the day after the new moon.

CASTING THE SPELL

1 Cast a circle in accordance with the guidelines on pages 32–35.

2 Light the tea-light, and heat the point of the nail in its flame.

3 Use the hot tip of the nail to inscribe into the side of the white candle, about 1"/2.5 cm from the wick, the outline of an eye.

4 Roll the paper bearing the signature into a tight scroll, and tie it to the center of the black cotton thread. Tie the scroll and thread around the candle, passing the thread over the center of the eye. Fasten it tightly.

5 Light the candle, saying:
[Name of suspect], if thou a liar be
Thou shalt find discovery
And all thy deeds be marked to thee
As I will it, so mote it be!

YOU WILL NEED

One tea-light in a holder

Matches or a lighter

One sharp iron nail

One white candle, 6–8"/15–20 cm in length

One slim piece of paper bearing the signature of the deceiver

One 6"/15 cm length of black cotton embroidery thread

Witness the candle burning down to consume the inscribed eye, the cotton thread, and the paper scroll.

6 Extinguish it, and bury it in earth where it will not be disturbed.

MIRROR IMAGE SPELL
TO CONFUSE AN ENEMY

PURPOSE This spell is designed to frustrate the plans of one who is doing you harm.

BACKGROUND Mirrors turn up in many spells all over the world, and they certainly have a reputation for mystery and magic. They symbolize the fine line between truth and illusion, because what they show is not always as simple as it seems. Perhaps this has something to do with the fact that a mirror can offer the illusion of space and entry to a three-dimensional world, when in fact it simply reflects what is in front of it as a two-dimensional object. Often a mirror can conceal as much

HOW TO CAST THE SPELL

YOU WILL NEED

One charcoal disk in a fireproof dish

One blue candle, 6–8"/15–20 cm in length

Matches or a lighter

One teaspoon of mugwort

Two identical circular mirrors approximately 4"/10 cm in diameter

One teaspoon of poppy seeds

One tube of strong glue

One spool of pliable wire

TIMING Weave this spell on the night of the full moon, mistress of both truth and illusion.

CASTING THE SPELL

1 Cast a circle in accordance with the guidelines on pages 32–35.

2 Light the charcoal, then the candle, saying:

Child of the moon
Element of water
Reflect, distract
Direction alter
Shine upon [Name of wrongdoer]
Make their steps falter.

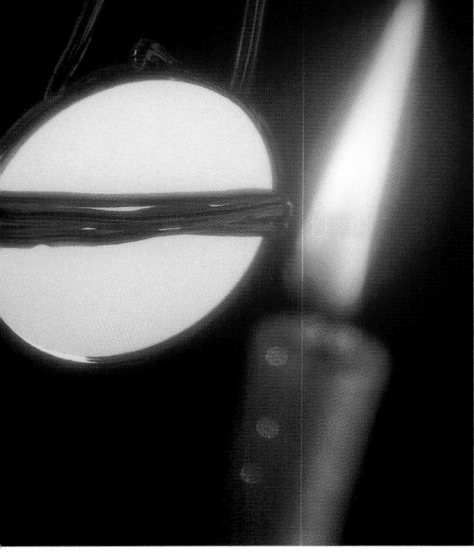

as it reveals, and in this spell it is this potential for confusion that is exploited in order to derail a troublemaker.

The tradition of placing a mirror in the window to deflect the evil eye relates to its ability to reflect, or bounce back, bad energy to its sender. Here, the mirrors are used to confuse and confound and also to radiate outward a shield against the bad intentions of the wrongdoer. The spell will create a double-sided mirror, which should be suspended over your front door outside the house. Ensure that all attachments are secure.

3 Sprinkle the mugwort onto the charcoal, take a mirror in each hand, then cense their reflective surfaces in the incense smoke, saying:

I hereby empower you
To show the truth.

4 Sprinkle on the poppy seeds, and repeat, saying:

I hereby empower you
To delude and confuse.

5 Firmly glue the backs of the mirrors together, and fasten the wire around and across the double-sided result, leaving a loop from which it can be suspended.

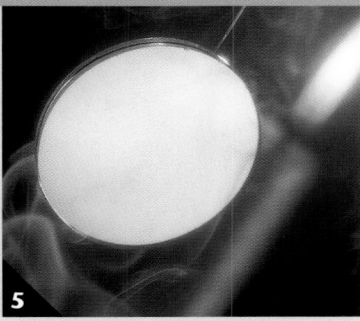

6 Hold this in front of the candle, saying:

Confusion to the enemy
As I have spoken
Let it be.

SEAT OF THORNS SPELL
TO RID YOURSELF OF A BULLY

PURPOSE   To remove a bully from power.

BACKGROUND   Bullying behavior comes in many forms and should always and without exception be challenged. It is not always easy for a person or a group of people who are being browbeaten to confront the bully who has already intimidated them, and this is why it is important to take practical steps in seeking outside help. If you are being intimidated by a housemate or a colleague at work, you need to seek help from the person leasing to you or from your union or personnel department, respectively. If you are being harassed and threatened in your own home by a partner, consult

HOW TO CAST THE SPELL

YOU WILL NEED

One black candle, 6–8"/15–20 cm in length

Matches or a lighter

One charcoal disk in a fireproof dish

Six large dried bramble thorns

Six dressmaker's pins

One small glass jar with a screw cap

TIMING Cast this spell at any time, but if you have a choice, plump for the waning moon, as this phase is best for carrying unwanted things away on the outgoing tide.

CASTING THE SPELL

1 Cast a circle in accordance with the guidelines on pages 32–35.

2 Light the candle, saying:
I cast you out
I sent you hence
Let none protect
And none defend
Your rule of force
Is hereby ended.

3 Light the charcoal burner. Place five of the thorns on the charcoal, and allow them to burn to ash.

a support group or agency, and get legal advice. It might seem strange to you that a book on spells should advise you to take these measures, but magic is built on resourcefulness, and this includes using common sense.

This said, magic has its part to play and has long been the resort of those who are feeling powerless in the face of adversity. This is why there are so many spells for protection and defense in the tradition! This spell should be used in tandem with the practical steps you should be taking to end the rule of the bully in question.

4 Place the pins in the jar, with the ashes from the burned thorns, saying:

I hold the means of your dismay
Until your cruelty goes away
As you are cruel
These thorns shall be
When you are kind
You'll kindness find.

5 Screw the lid to the jar tightly, and keep it in a safe place until the bully departs.

6 Place the remaining thorn within or beneath the seat—wherever it is less likely to be detected—of the chair that the bully sits on.

BIRD'S NEST SPELL
TO SEND BACK TO AN EVILDOER THE RESULTS OF THEIR ACTIONS

PURPOSE To ensure that a wrongdoer is faced with the consequences of their behavior.

BACKGROUND There is an old English saying that opines, "It's a poor bird that fouls its own nest." This sentiment refers to the stupidity of behaving badly too close to home, where you will suffer the consequences of your actions because of your proximity to the fallout from them. This magician holds no brief for behaving badly away from home either, but there is something in this that does hold true. If the results of deeds are presented back to the person responsible, they will have to suffer what others have had to suffer from them. As well as ensuring that the wrongdoer is left in no doubt as to how unpleasant it is to be on the receiving end of bad behavior, it will also make obvious to all around them just who is responsible for any trouble being caused. This offers an obvious choice to the miscreant: desist or make amends, and your troubles will cease!

For this spell you will need the remnants of an old nest. If you keep a nest box, you will probably already be familiar with the practice of clearing out last year's nests to make room for a new clutch of eggs in the spring. If not, you may have to beg this from a more experienced neighbor or make friends with the wardens at a local nature reserve. Try to keep the nest as intact as possible.

HOW TO CAST THE SPELL

YOU WILL NEED

One charcoal disk in a fireproof dish

One black candle, 6–8"/15–20 cm
in length

One white candle, 6–8"/15–20 cm
in length

Matches or a lighter

One teaspoon of dried juniper berries

One intact disused bird's nest

TIMING Cast on the dark moon, at the
turning of the moon's tide, to ensure that
the troublemaker in question receives
what they have given.

CASTING THE SPELL

1 Cast a circle in accordance with the
guidelines on pages 32–35.

2 Light the charcoal, then the black
candle to your left, saying:
The time of sending is gone.

3 Light the white candle, saying:
The time of return is near.

4 Sprinkle on the juniper berries.

5 Take the bird's nest in both hands and
hold it in the incense smoke, chanting the
following words:
After the flow comes the ebb
Everything we give we get
After the ebb comes the flow
Everything we get we know.

6 Place the bird's nest on your enemy's
doorstep secretly the same night.

WATER ELEMENTAL SPELL
TO MAKE VISIBLE TO OTHERS
THE ACTIONS OF AN EVILDOER

PURPOSE To unmask a wrongdoer and reveal their misdemeanors.

BACKGROUND Sometimes the worst punishment and best lesson for a troublemaker is exposure of their deeds. This will mean the loss of the good opinion of those they have been deceiving and will confront them with the inappropriateness or just plain unpleasantness of what they have been doing. Revealing the truth can also release those most affected by mischief from the frustration of being unable to prove what they know to be the case. This spell is also very useful in cases of mistaken

HOW TO CAST THE SPELL

YOU WILL NEED

One tea-light in a jar

Matches or a lighter

One stick of sandalwood incense

One drum

TIMING Cast on the night of the full moon at the side of a lake, sea, or river.

CASTING THE SPELL

1 Cast a circle in accordance with the guidelines on pages 32–35.

2 Light the tea-light in the jar. Stick the incense in the ground, and light it.

3 Using your hands, tap out a regular 3/4 rhythm, and allow your mind to follow the rhythm. When you feel ready, mentally reach out to the spirits of the water, and call them forth.

4 When you sense that the energies around you are changing significantly, speak over the drumming, repeating the following lines three times in succession:

Flowing mirror of the moon
Show [his/her] face in full
Show [him/her] as [his/her] true self
Show [him/her] in true form.

identity; if you are blaming the wrong person, all that is revealed is their innocence.

This spell requires you to work outdoors, near an expanse of water. You will be using a quite advanced magical technique—evocation—so it is wise to get some other magical experience before attempting this. You will need a drum for this spell, and some practice prior to casting it is essential. Beat a rhythm in 3/4 time, as this is usually effective with water elementals. When you go, leave a gift such as a flower, shell, or leaf cast at the water's edge.

5 Continue drumming for as long as you feel the water spirits around you. As the energies diminish, try to visualize the water flowing to the door of the person whose infamy you wish to reveal.

6 Leave a small gift at the waterside to honor the spirits of water.

INK WASH SPELL
TO CANCEL OUT HARM CAUSED BY ANOTHER

PURPOSE To be performed by the person who has been adversely affected by the dishonesty or poor behavior of another, as it has therapeutic as well as magical value.

BACKGROUND The impact of a troublemaker's conduct can be felt long after the original deed has taken place. This is part of the ongoing damage that irresponsible and dishonest people can cause, and it is as true for unwitting bystanders and dupes as it is for those who have been directly targeted. A person being unfaithful to their partner, for example, may leave behind not only an injured and angry ex-partner, but also a string of disappointed and very hurt friends and relatives who may have been enlisted, unwittingly, in their efforts to deceive. Similarly, friends, relatives, and partners of people who have been attacked also sustain damage by proxy—and have to deal with feelings of guilt, powerlessness, and anger.

In cases such as these, and in addition to very practical steps that can be taken to support the direct victims of violence or other unacceptable acts, this spell can help to diminish the residual effects of harm in a very therapeutic way. Many psychologists acknowledge the value of expressing pain through ritual. This spell may have originated many ages before psychology or the life of the mind was recognized professionally, but its methods nonetheless are recognizably therapeutic.

HOW TO CAST THE SPELL

YOU WILL NEED

One black candle, 6–8"/15–20 cm in length

Matches or a lighter

One bottle of purple water-based ink

One fountain pen

One sheet of office paper

One bowl of water

One small glass tumbler

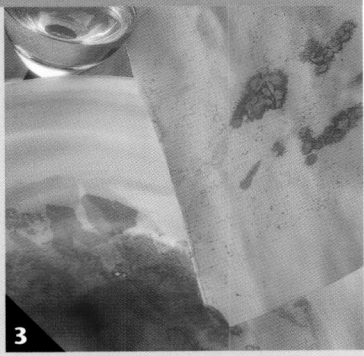

TIMING Cast on a waning moon, any time after the dark moon.

CASTING THE SPELL

1 Cast a circle in accordance with the guidelines on pages 32–35.

2 Light the candle, saying:
All that is valuable, I keep
All that is harmful, I discard.

3 Dip the nib of the pen into the water-based ink, and write on one side of the paper, in three words, the harm that has been done to you. Holding this over the bowl of water, and using the tumbler as a scoop, wash the ink from the page.

4 Dry the paper over the candle flame, taking care not to set it alight.

5 Write on the paper three words that represent positive and healing things to replace the harm you have washed away.

6 Dry the ink over the candle flame, then roll up the paper, and keep it for a year and a day. After this, burn it and scatter the ashes in your garden.

SEVERING SPELL
TO BREAK WITH THE PAST

PURPOSE To destroy the power that memories of past events have over you.

BACKGROUND This is another very therapeutic spell, best performed by the person who wishes to break with the past. If memories of past events still wield an unhealthy amount of power over us, then it is not healthy to allow this to continue. To release the past with a spell is not to trivialize pain or suffering that may have come from past events, but to ensure that the best outcome can be achieved. In any case, letting the past run riot in the present gives it undue space in our lives, and the more

HOW TO CAST THE SPELL

YOU WILL NEED

One charcoal disk in a fireproof dish

One black candle, 6–8"/15–20 cm in length

Matches or a lighter

One teaspoon of myrrh

One 9"/22.5 cm length of black cord

One fireproof dish

One pinch of saffron

TIMING Cast on the dark moon, a powerful time for endings and new beginnings.

CASTING THE SPELL

1 Cast a circle in accordance with the guidelines on pages 32–35.

2 Light the charcoal disc, then the candle, saying:

By this token I am freed and come toward the light.

3 Sprinkle the myrrh onto the charcoal.

4 Tie a knot toward one end of the cord: this represents the memories you wish to leave behind. Tie another knot toward the other end of the cord: this represents a future free from the feelings that are keeping you in the past.

attention we offer sadness, the more it will grow to block out our capacity for joy.

If you find that memories of a broken relationship, a bereavement, or traumatic events are still haunting you in a way that is not in keeping with the natural grieving process, then you should talk things through with a friend or counselor. If you wish to break with these feelings from the past, then this spell is absolutely ideal. At a psychic level, it severs your emotional links with the past to the extent that you will be able to live your life without those painful feelings.

5 Holding the "past" knot in your left hand and the "future" knot in your right, place the cord over the flame, and allow it to burn through. Burn the "past" knot entirely, placing it in the fireproof dish.

6 Place the saffron on the charcoal, and cense the knot that represents your future. Keep this in a safe place.

FIRE STAIN SPELL
TO FRUSTRATE ONE WHO IS DOING HARM TO OTHERS

PURPOSE To foil the plans of a wrongdoer.

BACKGROUND This spell is thought to originate from Scotland, but variations of it may be found in a number of European countries. It is based on an old form of ill-wishing reputedly used in circumstances such as illegal evictions, where families were removed from their homes by unscrupulous owners in order to sell property or land or to replace them with higher-paying tenants. It was the custom of the departing family, or at least those with some of the ancient knowledge, to leave stones in the fire grate in place of the usual coals, in order to wish the owner ill in return for their bad treatment. The wish is implicit: "May there be cold stones instead of hot coals at your hearth."

Leaving behind *stains*, as the Scots called them, was effectively a form of binding spell, to ensure that the wrongdoer's deeds would be returned to them. In this spell, you will be doing something very similar in order to frustrate the plans of one who intends to do harm to others. In this case, you will not need access to their fireplace, but you will reenact the fire stains tradition by building a cairn of special stones and leaving them in a pile on their wall or by their gate.

HOW TO CAST THE SPELL

TIMING Cast this spell the night before the dark moon, so that the stains are in place by the next morning.

CASTING THE SPELL

1 Cast a circle in accordance with the guidelines on pages 32–35.

2 Light the charcoal, then the candle. Place both palms against the sides of the candle, saying:

All that burns between these hands is all the warmth you will receive [Name of wrongdoer].

3 Sprinkle the rosemary onto the charcoal.

4 Sprinkle salt over all the pebbles, saying to each one:

Nothing shall grow of thee.

Pour water over all the pebbles, saying to each one:

Nothing shall be nourished of thee.

5 Now cense each pebble in the incense smoke, saying to each one:

No grace shall be received of thee.

Drip one drop of black wax onto each pebble from the candle.

6 Before morning, take the pebbles to the front gate or wall of the wrongdoer, and place them in a pile.

YOU WILL NEED

One charcoal disk in a fireproof dish

One black candle, 6–8"/15–20 cm in length

Matches or a lighter

One tablespoon of dried rosemary

One container of salt with a flow hole

Five palm-size pebbles, naturally smoothed by water

One wineglass of spring water

GLOSSARY

AMULET Strictly speaking, an item worn or displayed to attract certain energies such as luck, prosperity, health, love, and so on, but generally used as a term for a charm, often interchangeably with the term *talisman*.

ATHAME Witches' knife, used to direct magical energy.

BALEFIRE A fire used for magical purposes.

BELTAINE One of the eight Pagan festivals, celebrated traditionally from sundown on April 30 to sundown on May 1, or when the May tree is in bloom.

CHARGE To fill with magical energy or to entrust with a magical task.

CLADDAGH A traditional Irish village near a seashore where the claddagh design for a ring was used for centuries. It shows an Irish symbol of clasped hands, denoting true friendship, love, or amity.

CLOUTIES Rags or ribbons tied usually to a tree above a holy well, as an act of respect to a local deity or to symbolize a wish or hope.

CORN DOLLIES Items woven from ripe corn (wheat), charged with spiritual or magical meaning.

CUNNING MAN A traditional term for a man knowledgeable in magical and natural lore, and renowned for healing, dowsing, divination, or spell-casting powers.

DARK MOON The "new" moon phase, when the moon is completely overshadowed and invisible.

DEOSIL "Sun-wise"—meaning in a clockwise direction.

ELEMENT CANDLES Appropriately colored candles representing the five sacred elements.

EOSTRE One of the eight Pagan festivals, celebrated at the Vernal or Spring Equinox, usually March 21 or 22. The word derives from the Teutonic fertility goddess Oestra or Ostar.

FETCH A magical likeness of yourself, created magically and sent over a distance to appear to others.

LITHA One of the eight Pagan festivals, celebrated on the day of the Summer Solstice, or "longest day," which occurs on or around June 21.

LUGHNASADH One of the eight Pagan festivals, celebrated toward the end of July, around the time of the cereal harvest.

MABON One of the eight Pagan festivals, celebrated at the autumnal Equinox, on or around September 21, and sacred to the fruitful mother goddess who bears its name.

FITH-FATH Another name for a "poppet" or symbolic representation of a person. It is usually, though not always, in the form of a simple doll.

FIVE SACRED ELEMENTS The symbolic and physical aspects of all existence, divided into earth, air, fire, water, and spirit.

GOD-MAKING The formation of an item used as a protective charm, usually wooden and taking the energies of the tree from which it is sourced.

IMBOLC One of the eight Pagan festivals, sacred to the Celtic goddess Brigid, and traditionally celebrated on or around February 1, or at the emergence of the first snowdrops.

KNOTTING A technique used in magic to secure energy in a cord, which is sometimes released when the knot is untied.

MAGICIAN'S CORDS Cords used in spells for magical purposes, or as part of a spell.

MEASURE Traditionally lengths of cords that are measured directly from life, rather than a tape-measure; around the head, the heart, and the length of the body from head to toe—in short, shroud measurements—and thought to have a sympathetic connection with the person whose measurements are taken.

OUROBORUS An ancient symbol of eternity, depicting a snake swallowing its own tail.

PENTACLE A five-pointed star depicted with interwoven cross points visible. The sacred symbol of magic and elements conjoined, denoting the element of Earth, if encircled, or the element of spirit, if in its simple, five-pointed form. Traditionally, a distinction has been made between pentacle and pentagram, respectively a five-pointed star in a circle, or a star un-encircled, but sometimes this definition is reversed, and nowadays the terms are used with fairly careless interchangeability.

PHILTER A magical liquid, usually to be drunk.

POPPET A doll-like sachet made in order to represent a person for the purposes of a spell.

RUNE A figure from an ancient alphabet, originating from Northern Europe, and used for meditation, divination, or spell work to invoke an energy or meaning derived from its ancient origins, or in some cases to represent a person or situation for the purposes of magical work.

SACHET A small pillow sewn from fabric and stuffed with herbs or other materials.

SAMHAIN One of the eight Pagan festivals, celebrated on or around October 31, or when the first frosts set in.

SIDHE An Irish name for the faeries, or hill-folk.

SIGIL A mark or figure of magical relevance, used in a similar way to runes in magic.

SUN-RETURN Another name for the Winter Solstice, or "shortest day," which occurs on or around December 21.

SUN-WISE Clockwise, or *deosil*.

SYMPATHETIC MAGIC Sometimes called *like with like*, this is a system of magic that uses symbols to represent someone or something outside of themselves, and which may have a physical connection (i.e. hair, nail, or signature of the person in question) or a metaphorical or created one (a poppet or fith-fath). A spell-caster may then enact upon that symbol what they wish to happen to the person or something in everyday life.

TALISMAN Strictly speaking, this is a magical item worn or displayed by a person to ward off particular energies—for example, bad intents, jealousy, the evil eye, or bad luck—but is often used interchangeably with the word *amulet*. It is sometimes used simply to mean "charm."

TASSEOGRAPHY The art of reading tea leaves for divinatory purposes.

THOUGHT-FORM A magical form generated by your own thoughts and will, usually manufactured with the aid of a mirror.

TISANE Another word for a herbal tea, brewed with boiling water.

TRANSFERENCE Conveying a situation from one place to another by magical means. For example, transference occurs when a wart on a person is magically rubbed onto a stone, the stone is buried or thrown into deep water, and the wart disappears.

TRIPLICITIES The tendency, in magic, and in Celtic culture in particular, for symbols and supernatural or sacred beings to have a threefold aspect.

TRISKELE A Celtic symbol, originating in Brittany, depicting a three-legged spiral.

TRUE MIDNIGHT The middle point of the hours between sunset and sunrise.

TUMBLED Smoothed by a process of "tumbling." This term describes smoothed crystals or semi-precious stones.

WANING MOON The phase of the moon that sees its lit portion diminishing after the full phase until the dark or new moon phase; in the Northern Hemisphere the lit disc retains the circular curve on the left side, and appears to diminish from the right. This phase includes the last quarter, or waning half-moon.

WAXING MOON The phase of the moon following the new or dark phase and prior to the full phase. This phase sees the lit portion growing; in the Northern Hemisphere the lit disc retains the circular curve on the right side, and appears to grow from right to left. This phase includes the first quarter, or waxing half-moon.

WHEEL OF THE YEAR The solar year on Earth experienced as a cycle of seasons and change, and including the phases of sun, moon, stars, and nature.

WISEWOMAN A traditional term for a woman knowledgeable in magical and natural lore, and renowned for healing, dowsing, divination, or spell-casting powers—a witch.

YULE One of the eight Pagan festivals, celebrating the "shortest day" and held on or around December 21. Also known as *Sun-return*.

INDEX

M

N

R

Raspberry Leaf Sachet (for ease in childbirth) 174–175

Red Bracelet Spell (to bestow good fortune on a newborn baby) 296–297

relatives, keeping at bay troublesome 190–191

Ribbon Spell (to attract an exciting lover) 228–229

Ring of Roses Spell (to bless and protect a couple and their relationship) 326–327

Roman Cornucopia Spell (to bestow luck on a new home) 294–295

Rose Petal Spell (to summon true love) 50–51

S

sacred spaces 32–35

saffron 193

Salt and Water Spell (a self-blessing for times of trouble) 332–333

Samhain, 24, 30, 230, spells for, *see* Crone Spell 250–251, Gateway Spell 252–253, Tharf Cake Spell 254–255

Saturn 19

Sea Spell (to bring good health) 236–237

Seat of Thorns Spell (to rid yourself of a bully) 372–373

Seed Spell (to grow wishes and bring success in new projects) 214–215

self-esteem, building of 140–141

serpent 62, 159

Sesame Spell (to remove obstacles to your career) 108–109

Severing Spell (to break with the past) 380–381

Shield Spell (for protection in stressful situations) 330–331

Shoe Charm spell (to gain the notice of someone to whom you are attracted) 76–77

Sigil Spell (to aid with interview success) 100–101

Silver Candle Spell (to aid quick-wittedness in study and in the workplace) 112–113

sleep, aiding restful 162–163

Snakeskin Spell (to enhance the libido and pep up your love life) 62–63

Snapdragon Spell (to guard against spite) 306–307

solar cross 96

Solar Cross Charm (to find the correct career path) 96–97

ACKNOWLEDGMENTS

The Bridgewater Book Company would like to thank the following for the permission to reproduce copyright material:

Corbis pp. 18 background (Otto Rogge), 42/43 (Greenhalf Photography), 48/49 (Matthew Allen), 70/71 (Larry Williams), 76/77 (Rick Rappapart), 80/81 (Jens Haas), 96/97 (Owaki-Kulla), 109 (Jim Richardson), 118/119 (Michael St. Maur Sheil), 142 (Randy Faris), 154/155 (Anthony Cooper), 166/167 (Hanan Isachar), 168 (David Papazian), 175 (Steve Prezant), 182/183 (Matthew Allan), 184/185 (Leland Bobbé), 198/199 (James P. Blair), 210 (Matthew Kitto), 274/275 (Charles Krebs), 298/299 (Jennifer Kennard), 310/311 (Benjamin Rondel), 315 (Charles O'Rear), 316/317 (Raymond Gehman), 324 (Tim Pannell), 356 (Ralph A. Clevenger).
Marc Henri p. 64.